Dallas 5466
Limo George

BY GEORGE BENKER

DORRANCE
PUBLISHING CO
EST. 1920
PITTSBURGH, PENNSYLVANIA 15238

The contents of this work, including, but not limited to, the accuracy of events, people, and places depicted; opinions expressed; permission to use previously published materials included; and any advice given or actions advocated are solely the responsibility of the author, who assumes all liability for said work and indemnifies the publisher against any claims stemming from publication of the work.

Dorrance Publishing Co
585 Alpha Drive
Pittsburgh, PA 15238
Visit our website at *www.dorrancebookstore.com*

ISBN: 978-1-6470-2458-1
eISBN: 978-1-6470-2706-3

Dallas 5466
Limo George

⊗　　　⊗　　　⊗　　　⊗　　　⊗

*Y*ou might be asking yourself, 'Who is Limo George?'

I actually met George in 2011. We have been friends now for approximately 8 years. During our friendship, George had told me a number of these stories that I found very entertaining and interesting. He expressed a desire to put them in a book. At that time, I would have never dreamed I would be the one who actually put his stories into written form to be able to go into a book! *Dallas 5466* is his dream come true!

But Who Is Limo George? My first impression of George was that he was a big ol' teddy bear. He had a big infectious smile, a twinkle in his eyes, an indomitable spirit, and a heart of gold! He would help anyone at any time! I believe that his list of priorities goes as follows: Jesus Christ his Savior, his wife, his children and grandchildren....and then it would be a tie between America....and Dallas, Texas! George would tell anyone in a heartbeat that he bleeds red, white, and blue!

The stories George has chosen for his book are just the tip of the iceberg! They are some of the best stories that depict some of the funniest and most interesting people and events he experienced during his 30 years owning a limo company in the great city of Dallas, Texas, and the areas all around Ft. Worth as well! I feel certain that you will enjoy sharing the "ride" along with Limo George as he takes you in the limo....or, maybe the party bus for the ride of your life!

But, before you get started...go put on some comfy clothes, get yourself a tasty snack, settle into your favorite chair...and enjoy the ride...with Limo George and Dallas 5466!

I am here today honoring my best friend of over 20 years and his lovely new bride!

George and I have been there through so many great times, great laughs, and some challenging moments. Through it all, he has had advice and perspective during the times when I struggled for some!

A quick list of some of the fun times:

- Tons of Byron Nelson's, Cowboy games, and Concerts
- Sharing a love for the theater and even going to Mama Mia 2 nights in a row!
- Dressing up and playing Santa at the Elementary School
- Taking Brandon and Katelyn to the mall on weekends
- Shopping at Jeffs store and filling the limo trunk
- Hanging at Mondo's, Trulucks, and Steve Fields
- Dressing up as Austin Powers
- Christmas light tours with Neil crawling on the limo floor and peeing in Highland Park
- Ordering a Limo for a Christmas Light tour and G showing up with a Hot Pink Barbie Bus with a stripper pole
- Brandon's birthday parties
- Starting a business together
- Being my protector on my late nights out
- A multitude of rides to the airport at 3:00 in the morning - never late or wrinkled!
- Loosing someone following us in a stretch limo - don't know how you did it!

And some of the challenging moments:

- Picking me up on the tollway when my new Lexus engine blew
- Moving a co-worker out and back into his house in one day with Ana's help when the guy said he was moving in with me
- Working out together and G puking
- Rehab and G puking
- Long bedside chats after G's surgery and in rehab
- Picking up a Christmas gift from a cheating boyfriend that didn't deserve what I gave him
- Taking me to purchase a diamond ring and telling me I didn't need a cheating boyfriend
- And the biggest one of al...being there with me at court when I lost custody of Brandon

As you can tell, these are not all the stories that George and I could tell of our years of friendship, so you will have to read George's book!

Through the 20+ years that I been best buddies with George, we have laughed and cried together. I always know, though, that if I want to see his eye's sparkle, I have him talk about his family. He glows when he talks about his children, grandchildren, and great grandchildren. Now, with Kathy joining the family, I see a "Sparkle and Smile" that is bigger and brighter than ever. I am so happy for these beautiful and deserving newlyweds. We love you both!

LIMO
Dallas 5466

I was in the Limo business for 30 years and have met many interesting people, and groups of people! I have gotten to share "special life moments" with more people at more places than I could ever remember! Some of the places I have been privileged to go have blown my mind and I'm sure if you could have been there, they would have blown your mind as well!

This unexpected career choice has led down a path of events I could never have imagined in my wildest dreams! The life lessons I have learned along the way have been immeasurable and somewhat overwhelming at times! I have grown not only as a man, but also as a human being because of the many wonderful and sometimes not so wonderful people I have met along this 30 year journey.

All of these stories are true. None are made up! All of the people in the stories are real people. Some of the names have been changed to protect the "innocent!" Some were changed because I couldn't remember them clearly after all these years, but they were real live people!

If you are mentioned by name in this book, you were/are exceptional! You made your mark in my heart and mind. If you think you see your story in the book and I didn't mention your name...that may be a good thing! You still made a lasting impression on me!

Many of these stories will make you laugh, some may even bring a tear to your eye, and some of them may have historical importance relating to Dallas/Ft. Worth. Whatever your reaction is, I hope for this book is that it makes you smile and gives you a better understanding of the people, places, and things around the amazing place called Dallas!

What about the title of the book you may ask. I'm sure you already know what the LIMO part is about, but what is Dallas 5466? Keep reading...I'll tell you soon! I stumped my assistant!! Can you guess what it is?

Two Valentines

I wanted to tell you how Valentine's Day celebrations turned out at opposite ends of the spectrum based on....words....sweet words... or dumb words!

I picked up the first couple at their house. Actually from looking at them they really looked like a couple in love. First I took them for a lovely dinner at a swanky restaurant in Dallas. There was lots of toasting with champagne and giggling and laughing going on. When they got back to the limo, the lady wanted to go dancing. So, they decided on a club and off we went to finish dancing the night away! Again, they seemed very much in love. There was lots of slow, snuggly dancing and loud laughing and partying! When they were ready to go home, they piled back in the limo for the trip home! Instead of winding down, the booze seemed to have wound the guy up. He didn't really seem ready for the night to end. However, the lady was fading fast! Unfortunately, Mr. Macho was determined he wanted to end the night with sex in the limo! His lady was determined that was not going to happen! She moved over to the seat by me. In a moment, I could only imagine that he lunged at her and she kicked him in a very strategic spot between his legs! He hollered in pain and started cussing. Luckily, we were pulling up to their house about that time. He stumbled out of the limo and into the house in pain! She just sat there stunned! In a minute he came storming back out with a suitcase and screams, "You never do anything I want to do. I don't know why I have stayed with you as long as I have!" He jumped in his car and spun out of the driveway and sped away. When the lady finally came to her senses, she got out of the limo and had to go in the house to try and find money to pay me! What started out as a couple in 'love' ended up with one leaving and one left hurt and confused!!

The second Valentine's story is about a group of friends getting together to celebrate the Day of Love as a group…in twos! I started picking up the participants with the original couple and then I wound around the neighborhood to pick up the rest of the couples. It was a group of 8 people, or 4 couples. As usual, there was lots of laughing and talking! I could tell by the happy chatter that they were all enjoying the dynamics of the group! The first stop was for dinner at a nice restaurant. On nights like this where my clients are eating, I usually take the opportunity to eat at the restaurant myself and I get to observe the group. You can learn a lot by just watching how people interact with each other.

After dinner, the next stop was to go to a club for some drinking and dancing. The night went as planned and everyone seemed to be having lots of fun! When it was finally time to end the night, we started the process of dropping all the couples off one by one. As each couple got out, they started teasing the first couple that they would soon have the limo to themselves! When I let the 3rd of the 4 couples out, they really grinned and teased the last couple about having the limo to themselves!

When that 3rd couple got out, there was a sparkle in the last guy's eyes. When I got back in the front, he called up to me and said, "George, could we ride around for a little while?" I told him, "Sure!"

As I began driving around the area, after a few minutes, I could tell the limo was 'rocking' a little bit more than it usually did! I smiled! This Valentine's Day was ending…just right!

And…what happens in the limo…stays in the limo! (Wink)

Which One to Choose...

I had been a home builder in the Dallas area for a number of years and when the housing market started into a slump, I decided I needed to begin to look for another more profitable business direction. A friend of mine was already in the limo business and I decided that might be an interesting business to get into for myself.

He let me work for him a couple of months to get the feel for the business to see if it was going to be a good fit for me. I must admit, it was a complete 180 degrees different from the home building industry! I decided the limo business might really be a fun business to be in!

Before you start any business you have to do your due diligence. I began my research to discover which cars made the very best limos. My research led me to the Cadillac limos!

BUT....before I tell you *why* the Cadillacs were the best limos....let me ask you a question.....how are limos made? Are there factories that just make limos? NO! A limo starts out as a regular car. The chassis is cut in half and extra chassis pieces are welded between the original front and back pieces and reinforced. At that point the center part is then made into what is now the beginning of the new limo!! The *new limo* then is made into a luxurious work of art!

I digress! Cadillac limos had the edge over other limo models for several reasons including being wider, they were more powerful, better looking, and most of all, they had a better warranty of 100,000 miles (which is needed for being in constant use)! Two other important factors in Cadillac's favor was they had great air conditioners (which is a *must* for the Texas heat), and better electrical systems which also helped eliminate break downs during the heat of the Texas summers!

I started out with 1 Cadillac limo and 6 months later I was able to get my second one! Things were looking really good for my limo business in Dallas. *I loved my Cadillac limos!!*

Unfortunately, after being in business about 5 or 6 years, Cadillac switched over to making front wheel drive automobiles and stopped making Cadillacs that could be converted into limos. What a waste! I, like the rest of the limo world, had to switch to Lincoln limos. Since the time Cadillac stopped making limos several other companies have tried their hand at making limos, including Hummer, *but the Cadillac, in my opinion was the Gold Standard!*

Limos and Party Buses:

One of the many benefits of being in the limo business is that you get to meet a lot of different people from all walks of life and many of them can and will become business partners in one form or another. One partnership that formed involved Party Buses. We found we were able to buy small transport buses from the airport that they used to move passengers from one terminal to another at very reasonable prices when it was time to turn over their inventory. They were low mileage and well maintained. It was a win-win for everyone involved. We would purchase a bus, tear everything out on the inside, and convert them into 'Party Buses'!

They would be complete with lighting systems, and rocking audio systems and really cool and stylish interiors. They were perfect for small parties and the party could stay in one place and travel! The party buses could also be used for tailgating, transportation to proms, or a number of other fun destinations! The Party Bus was definitely a big addition to the limo business!

Woman Up

*I*n the summer of 1995, my business was growing and flourishing! Late one evening I was waiting to pick up my next clients when I received a call from a lady named Mary. Mary had been driving for the Dallas Area Transit and she wanted to make a change to driving limousines. I asked her a few probing questions about her driving experience since driving a longer vehicle takes more attention, especially to turning corners and backing up. She had not had any moving traffic violations, so I decided to meet with Mary to see if she would be a good fit for my company.

Mary was a tall, slender woman whose appearance gave the impression she could probably handle herself in a crisis. I wouldn't say Mary was pretty, but the **quote *'a face only a mother could love'*** did come to mind! I'm sure Mary's mother **really** loved her! After a lengthy sit-down conversation with Mary, I decided to give Mary a chance.

Her first clients were a group of Hispanic couples who were out to celebrate one of their birthdays! They hired us to take them around to a number of Hispanic/Latin clubs as part of their celebration! I spoke with Mary a number of times during the first 3 hours of the fare and everything was going great! There was lots of laughter, partying...and 'stimulants'!

About 1 o'clock, I got a frantic call from Mary saying the limo had just died! She could not get it to crank or get the engine to turn over. They were stranded at a corner in downtown Dallas in a not so good area of town! I had just dropped off my last clients for the night and I assured Mary I was on my way!

When I arrived in about half an hour, I found the 'party' still going on with her Hispanic clients. They had exited the limo and were continuing to dance and drink on the sidewalk! Since they were still having fun, I opened up the hood and worked to get the limo back on the road. About the time I finished getting the limo fixed, 3 or 4 Dallas police cars came swooping in and blocked my limo! The police all jumped out of their cars with their guns drawn and running towards our clients! Mary and I were stunned to say the least! Our clients didn't seem to notice for the first few seconds as they continued to laugh and dance!

The police, with guns drawn, started to yell for them all to get up against the fence that was next to the sidewalk! *That finally got their attention!* Then the policemen started asking for all of their identification. By this time, I was able to ask one of the police what was going on. He said several people had called complaining about the noise they were causing in the neighborhood. By this time, the gravity of the situation had finally started to sink in with my clients.

By now, 6 of the people had been handcuffed and were being taken to the police cars. It seemed 3 of the 6 had warrants out on them, and the other 3 were in possession of marijuana and cocaine! While all of this excitement and confusion was going on, I had motioned for Mary to get in her limo and quietly leave and that I would call her in a little while. With the development of finding drugs on the people, the police asked to search 'the limo'. Of course, I immediately gave them permission and complied…since the limo they had been partying in was the one Mary had left in. As I suspected, nothing was found in the limo!

With those 6 people being arrested, that left the other 4 of the women! After the police left with the 6 people who were being arrested, the 4 women that were left were almost hysterical! In a few minutes I called Mary to come back. She had these 4 ladies' purses in her limo. When Mary got there, she picked up the ladies and we all headed to the Police Department to bail the 6 men out of jail! It took until almost mid-morning before we were able to return our clients back to their car.

What a *night!* Oddly enough, Mary decided she didn't really want to drive a limo after all!!

Mary was my *FIRST* and *LAST* woman driver!

1st Flat Tire on the Limo

*I*n driving a limo for 30 years, I only had a flat tire 1 time. However, on that 1 time I had 2 flat tires! I guess if you're going to have a first time it might as well be a memorable one!

I was driving a couple around for their anniversary and they were drinking champagne and having a good time! It's always nice to see people actually enjoying their anniversary! During my time in driving limos, I have seen some anniversary celebrations start out really well, that did not end well! But this couple seemed really in love and were having themselves some fun!

As I'm quietly cruising around, suddenly I realize that I have run over something in the road and my tire is going flat! I stop the car and call back to tell them that I think we have a flat tire, but it's okay, for them to just keep enjoying themselves!

I left all of the electrical on so they would have lights and air conditioning and remain comfortable. When I got out to check my tire, I had 2 flat tires and I only had 1 spare! I called AAA to bring me another tire and to help change the tires.

I went ahead and jacked the car up on one side to start removing one tire while I was waiting for them to get there. Everything was going well for a while...until the *limo started shaking*! I was startled at first until I realized *why the limo was shaking*! Then, I started getting concerned, what if the jack slipped and the car dropped down! (You've heard the expression, *'If the car is rockin' don't come knockin''*!) I had a dilemma! I hated to disturb them, but I also hated for the jack to break and the car to fall with them in it! What should I do? I said a quick prayer and decided **NOT** to knock on the door! *They* *might not have heard me anyway!*

It wasn't long before the AAA guy got there, we got the tires changed, and we were back on the road!

That night was memorable for them because 'love' happened in the limo. It was memorable for me for 2 reasons: the first was what I call a 'God' thing because the jack didn't break and the car didn't fall, and the second thing was that it was the first and only time I ever had a (2) flat tire(s) in 30 years! God is GOOD!!

A 'Circular' Prom

*I*t didn't take me long to realize that the limo business was going to be full of surprises! And, that those surprises could come at any time and in any 'shape' you can imagine....or not imagine!

Prom nights were always some of my favorite bookings. They normally had some similarities and some things that were not similar at all. I call this A Circular Prom because it was one of my most unusual prom nights!

My instructions were to drive to the rear entrance of the school...which was out in the middle of Nowhere, Texas, and ask for Mrs. Jordan! I didn't have any trouble finding the school, or the rear entrance, but I was curious as to why I was making a 'pick-up' where I should have been 'delivering' the students to!

When I arrived at the 'rear' entrance to the school, it seemed kind of deserted except for a large number of cars already parked in the school parking lot. I got out of the limo and looked around wondering where I might find Mrs. Jordan. **Luckily, Mrs. Jordan found me!** I must admit, my curiosity was getting the best of me!

Mrs. Jordan was an attractive, forty-something year old woman who I quickly realized was the teacher in charge of the prom! As we got closer to the school building, and the door was slightly open, I could hear the chatter of excited voices!!! Even at this point, I still didn't get 'IT'! At last, Mrs. Jordan told me that each group would come out the back entrance of the school and get in the limo. I was to drive them around to the front where their parents would take pictures and they would enter the prom! At the end of the prom, I would drive each group from the school, down the main street in town to the Dairy

13

Queen, and back to the school! This would have been a slow ride of about 15 minutes all together, but I decided to make it a 'real limo ride' and made it a 30 minute round trip! Each group of kids still had some memorable moments of their prom night!

I had to give it to Mrs. Jordan, she made prom night in a small town into a night the students would remember....complete with a limo ride to the prom and home (with a detour by the Dairy Queen)!

Even though it was one of my most unusual prom night bookings, it was also one of my most gratifying...getting to add fun and exciting memories in a small town and school for prom night!!

Aerosmith & The Rolling Stones

*A*t Texas Motor Speedway!
Unfortunately, most people go through life without having very much excitement to look forward to. But for me, even before I started my limo business some 30 years ago, I had already realized that I was very blessed. However, one night out at the Texas Motor Speedway, I realized that dreams really *do* come true!

I had the pleasure of being one of the limo companies that had been hired to take the bands Aerosmith and the Rolling Stones out to Texas Motor Speedway for a shared concert. I was lucky enough to be allowed to help the "security" team during the concert and escorted the band members onto the stage. Being the lucky man that I am, I took that opportunity to sit on the steps while they performed to watch them...and of course, to make sure no fans tried to sneak up onto the stage! (Fortunately, they had *no* idea what a huge fan that I was!)

I couldn't believe that two of my favorite bands of all time were performing on the same stage and that I was getting to see them from the stage steps... and it didn't cost me a dime!! As a matter of fact...I was being *paid* to be there! **What kind of _sweet_ deal was that?** Only Limo George could land a deal like that...or at least that's what I was thinking at the time!

Steven Tyler and Aerosmith were crazy amazing as usual. Then the Rolling Stones came on stage..and then it happened! They sang the song that had been my *"national anthem"* during my high school years....**_I CAN'T GET NO, SA-TIS-FACT-ION!!! As far as I was concerned...Limo George had_** *just won the <u>lottery</u>!!*

The rest of the night was just one happy blur! Even after we took the band members back to their hotels, I was still on cloud 9! I think it took me about 3 days to finally get back to normal...well, I'm not sure that I ever got back to *"normal,"* but then again...***<u>who is really normal?</u>***

All for One and One for All!!
Prom Night!

*M*ost young people start looking forward to prom night long before they are even allowed to attend a prom night! When that time starts getting near, hours, days, weeks, and even months-worth of time is put into the planning of *the "perfect" night!*

In the old days, the prom night consisted of getting dressed up in fancy clothes, corsages and boutonnieres, a nice dinner….and then, *the dance!!* That's definitely *not* the picture anymore! Details of current prom nights now include hotel reservations for getting dressed, photographers for pictures, professional hair and make-up, fancy (often expensive) clothes, and the list goes on! *Of course, I can't complain because now…riding in a limo is a big part of the festivities!!*

I typically would start booking prom nights in January or February of the year. I made sure that I told the person or persons doing the booking the event what my requirements were as far as what I expected in regard to the "personal conduct" of all those I was transporting! While my company was booked for several hundred prom nights during the years, a particular group comes to mind!

Since I was driving the group that night, I was to pick up the 10 students at the Omni Hotel in Dallas at 5:30 P.M. The proud parents were gathered with the excited participants in the lobby of the hotel! I had the parents and students gather around to make sure *everyone* knew the rules!

RULE 1: No Alcohol!

RULE 2: No Drugs!

RULE 3: If you get to Rule 3, refer back to Rules 1 and 2!

17

There were some other behavioral rules of common courtesies, but basically, Rules 1 and 2 were primary! It was a tremendous responsibility to be in charge of the welfare and safety of unchaperoned kids for any length of time let alone at night....when they want to party!!

With the Rules out of the way, they were ready to get the party started!! They all loaded up and we were off on prom night!! Our first stop was a nice restaurant for dinner. Everyone enjoyed the food and fun at the restaurant! After leaving the restaurant, we were headed to the venue for the prom. About 20 minutes into the drive, one of the kids knocked on the window between the front of the limo and the back to get my attention. I opened the window and I was told a couple of them had forgotten their "tickets" to the prom and they couldn't get in without them. We had to go back to the hotel for them to get their tickets!!! Since this wasn't *my first prom*, I assured them that they would be able to get in without the tickets! They all began begging and pleading with me to go back to get the tickets! I eventually got a call from one of the parents making the same plea for me to return to the hotel for the "forgotten tickets." I finally relented and headed back to the Omni..

As I expected, when we reached the hotel, *all* of them scrambled out of the limo and headed for the elevators! I told them to hurry back!

You guessed it, they didn't return for about 25 minutes! I could see a discernable difference in some of their appearances between the time they went upstairs and when they returned. Some shirts were untucked, some makeup was smeared, and several looked a bit disheveled! They all piled back into the limo and the trip began....again!

We finally arrived at the school....and the *prom began*!! However, after about 45 minutes a couple of the kids (Susie and Jordan) came back to the limo. I let them in. A few minutes passed and the rest of the kids came back to the limo...accompanied by the principal and a couple of teacher chaperones! I got out of the car to see what was going on. The principal told me that, Alexis, Robert, Macey, and Juan had been suspected of drinking alcohol in the janitor's closet and they could smell liquor on their breath! It seemed that Susie and Jordan had come back because they knew what was about to happen and they wanted to avoid being asked to leave the prom in front of their friends!

Obviously, Alexis, Robert, Macey, and Juan didn't think Rules 1 and 2 applied when they weren't in the limo! Because of the actions of 4, the entire party-of-10 got sent home! The parents had been notified.

Why did I take all 10 of the kids back to the hotel? They had all been entrusted to my care for their safe trip to and from the prom. If I had left any of them there, I would have been in breach of my contract for both ends of their trip.

Some of the parents arrived back at the hotel about the same time we did. Others arrived shortly thereafter. Needless to say, the night had not turned out as planned after all the weeks of planning! As luck would have it, some of them were even angry with me...as if it was my fault their kids were kicked out of the prom!! In light of the outcome of the night, I reiterated the terms of our contract...including Rules 1, 2, and 3!

The kicker of the whole night was that a couple of the parents called me the next morning, pretty much demanding that I come to the school to tell the authorities that I *had not seen their child* consuming liquor! *and*, they wanted their money back for my services! I *politely* declined *both requests!*

Arlington National Cemetery

*I*t was always my honor to be able to take the family of one of our fallen soldiers to Arlington National Cemetery in Grand Prairie, Texas, for their funeral. I have the utmost respect for the men and women who have not only fought for our country and its freedoms, but who have also given the ultimate sacrifice for all of us who proudly call the United States of America our home. Too often we forget that not only do the service members themselves serve and sacrifice for our freedoms, but their families are sharing in their service and sacrifice as well.

The spouses and children, moms and dads, and other loved ones of the service members must endure the months and sometimes years away from home while they protect and serve.

So, it was my honor to be able to show my respect, not only to the fallen soldier, but to their grieving family as well by offering my service to them for free during this time of grief.

Even at such a somber time, I was always in awe at the beauty and precision of the military funerals. Everything was timed to an exact moment. Every car had its appointed time to pull up for the guests to exit and again to re-enter after the service.

Something that never failed to almost move me to tears was the row after row of white crosses that represented a single service member that had at one time or another served to protect this great country of ours. While all of them may not have died in combat, their service was still what the building blocks of our freedom was built on.

I have recently seen a post on Facebook that rings true with me and I'm sure with many of my fellow Americans that simply said, **"Until you are willing to risk coming home in a casket draped with an American flag, you don't have the right to dishonor it!"**

To me, it will always be about: Our Flag – Our Country (the greatest country in the world) – and Freedom!

Bachelor Party-Shreveport

I was blessed to be in the limo business for 30 years and to wear the title of Limo George for all that time. It was a title that I wore with great pride because it was a name that became well respected and often loved!

During those 30 years there were lots of unexpected unbelievable things that happened that included lots of laughs and lots of tears (mostly tears of joy)! I met a lot of interesting people: people you have heard of and people you haven't heard of. I was behind the scenes at many events that you can't even imagine getting to be at! During those years, at times I almost had to pinch myself to make sure I wasn't dreaming because of the people I got to meet and the things I got to do! Just incredible!

I did hundreds of bachelorette parties and bachelor parties and I could almost tell you beforehand some of the things that were going to happen *before* the party started! The bachelorettes had certain things they always did…and bachelors had pre-determined parties in which they knew what the other ones had done!

One trait about *all* bachelor parties is that the minute they got into the limo, they started pushing the buttons! They pushed every button in the back that included the lights, radio, stereo, moonroof, DVDs, and the windows! I would always tell them that the only button they *could not push was the 'E' button!* They would all laugh and acknowledge my request!

A particular bachelor party comes to mind about a group that I took on a once in a life time trip to Shreveport, Louisiana! I picked them up on Friday morning to start their fun and exciting weekend! By the time we reached Shreveport, we had already made numerous stops for bathroom breaks and puke breaks! Unfortunately, when there is a lot of alcohol being consumed with a relatively small amount of food, a lot of it tends to come back up! However, I was used to this scenario so it was par for the course!

When we arrived at our destination, I discovered that they had not made reservations at a hotel. We then had to drive around until we could find rooms for the next two nights. After having lunch, we went to the casinos for a while and then everyone was ready to ***return to the hotel…where they all passed out…on a Friday night…during the bachelor party!***

Saturday was better. We went to the casino again and after lunch they wanted to go to the strip clubs, which we did. Most men know that the entertainers at these clubs are very skilled saleswomen. They know what the men are anticipating and that is exactly what they are going to give them!

Around 7 or 8 o'clock about half of the guys decided they were ready to go back to the hotel. Since we were only about a mile from the hotel, they decided they were going to walk! Yes, I said, *walk*! So, I had 5 drunks walking the streets of Shreveport and 5 drunks still being entertained at the strip club! What a night this was turning out to be!

About an hour later, I got a call from one of the 5 guys that was walking to the hotel…and just as I had feared, they were lost! I had to gather up the guys at the club and go in search of the 5 lost in downtown Shreveport! I have to admit that that was a first for me to have to be picking up drunks off the street in a strange town!

When we got back to the hotel, everyone passed out again! The next morning when we all met for breakfast and got ready to return to Dallas, we realized we were 1 man short! The *groom* was missing! The guys started calling him, and calling him, and calling him, and about an hour later he finally answered! He had "fallen" in love with one of the dancers and she had taken him home with her!!!! He was the *groom*!!!

We got the address and had to drive to the other side of Shreveport to pick him up! Of course, that put us late leaving to return to Dallas! And, that made us late getting back to Dallas where the wives and girlfriends were waiting for us!

The funniest thing to me is how during the bachelor parties the guys act so rough and tough until they get back around their wives or girlfriends and then they are like little puppies! (They are all the same!)

Bachelor Party-Stolen Limo

his is the one and only story about a bachelor party that ended like this one! I must say that I am exceedingly thankful for that!

The night began as most bachelor parties began and that was with a trip to a restaurant for dinner and drinks…and more drinks, and then off to the gentlemen's club! What was unusual about this particular night was that by the time we got to the club, we already had one participant that had passed out in the back of the limo! Most guys at bachelor parties last a good bit longer than that!

Just to be the nice guy that I am, when I went inside to get the other guys situated to start having fun, I left the motor of the limo running and the air conditioner on for the drunk in the back! Since I had some influence in the club, I wanted the guys to get the best seats and service! But you can't even imagine my shock and dismay when I opened the door of the club to go back to the limo…*it was gone!!!*

At first, I couldn't believe my eyes! I closed my eyes and opened them back up hoping I wasn't seeing what I thought I was seeing! But it was gone! I rushed outside and looked up and down the street hoping it had just rolled a little bit! Nope! It was *gone!*

I called the police to report it stolen by a drunk driver. Then I started calling other limo companies in the area to get them to be on the lookout for my limo! I also called another one of my limo drivers that was in the area to come pick me up! When he arrived, we drove to the place I had originally picked them up from to see if he had gone back there, but he wasn't there! Then we decided to go back to the club to see if he might have returned there! As we turned the corner, I spotted my limo!

I don't know if I was more relieved or angry at that moment! When we pulled up, I jumped out of the car, pulled the guy out of the limo, and shook him! I was showing my anger toward him which is something I usually don't do! By the time I sat him back down in the driver's seat, I realized his face was bloody and his eye was swollen! To my surprise, I had no idea how that happened to his face! The next thing I noticed when I looked down, I saw that he had wrecked the side of my limo! About that time the police drove up! I told them I wanted to press charges against him for stealing and wrecking my car! They did arrest him for driving while intoxicated and for auto theft.

He got 10 years of probation and had to pay restitution to me for the damage done to my car. His brother was one of the guys in the bachelor party and he signed an agreement with me to make payments for the restitution. It took them 2 years to repay the damage!

So, the moral to this story is, no matter how nice you are and want to be, *do not leave the keys in your car when there is still a drunk in it!* They may not be as "out" as you think they are!

Bachelorette Party

o me, bachelorette parties were more fun and interesting than bachelor parties! Why? Women tend to get silly and funny when they start drinking and men...well, they tend to get mean and want to start fights. Not *all* women are like that...and of course, not *all* men are like that, but as a general rule when I picked them up to party that was generally what happened!

A lot of the bachelorette parties would start out with the women wearing some sort of sexual toys or items on their heads or dangling around their necks as a means to embarrass the bride. ***Sometimes that <u>did not work</u>....<u>the bride would do something to embarrass them!!</u>*** That's when the real fun would begin!

Quite often the bachelorette parties would head toward the LeBare club in Dallas! That was the "lady's club" in Dallas which was equal to the "gentlemen's clubs" for the men! This club had the top exotic male dancers that were sure to bring out the "party" in women of *any* age!

I had taken so many bachelorette parties there, that I was probably one of the very few men that were actually allowed into the club. I got to witness first-hand what was going on inside! I have to admit...it was rather eye-opening! The difference between the exotic male dancers and me was like comparing Mickey Mouse to the Hulk!!

As the ladies entered the club, they would cash out their larger bills for one dollar bills to make the "fun" last longer! Another interesting thing was that the men actually put on a show! They dressed up as different characters (cowboys, super heroes, etc.) and put on a show to the music! After their show, they would go down off of the stage and "visit" among the women and "dance" and talk to the individuals and groups! Of course, this is where they got their Speedos filled up with one dollar bills!

It was so much fun to watch the really shy ones come out of their shell as the night went on! By the time LeBare closed, there were very few if any "shy" women left!!

The ride home always seemed to be louder and more fun than the ride to the club. Everyone may have had a little (or a lot) too much to drink, and laughed themselves into exhaustion...but it would definitely be a night the bride would never forget. None of those lucky enough to have been a part of the party would ever forget it either!

Another thing I liked about the LeBare bachelorette parties was whatever one dollar bills they had left after leaving the club....they usually gave to *me!*

As for me...some bachelorette parties may have been a little more memorable than others, but each one represents the love between friends and the beginning of a new life for two people in love!!

Bachelorette Party-Bar Hopping

his is yet another bachelorette party gone wrong! Well, at least part of it went wrong!

I was taking a bachelorette party of 10 ladies out to celebrate the upcoming nuptials of one of them. We started the party in Lower Greenville, which is one of the entertainment areas of Dallas. Everyone was drinking and having a great time. The group was having fun bar hopping! I was just sitting in the limo watching for them to come out of one bar so we could go to another one when one of the ladies approached me about taking one of them home.

It seems that Mary was drunk (already) and they wanted me to take her home. It was around midnight, so I agreed. I asked what area she lived in and they told me and it was actually some distance from where we were. However, I decided that at that time of the night, the traffic might not be too bad so I could take her home and then come right back and pick them up.

Remember, Mary was drunk! They put Mary in the limo and pointed us in the direction of her apartment. They gave me the general vicinity and Mary was to direct me once we got there! Wrong! Have you ever tried to wake up a really drunk person let alone get information or directions out of them? _**That was almost mission impossible!**_ We went to 2 or 3 different apartment complexes before we found the right one! Once we found the complex, _**I realized her apartment was on the 2nd floor!**_

I was able to get Mary to wake up enough to give me her apartment key, but she could not stand up to walk!! So, guess who has to put this drunk woman, dressed to the hilt over his shoulder to carry her up a flight of stairs to her apartment?! That would be me!

Luckily, she did give me the correct key to her apartment! I took her inside and found her bedroom, plopped her on the bed, and covered her up! I told her I was leaving her keys on the coffee table and I left!

By this time, the rest of the bachelorette party had been calling me trying to see where I was and when I would be back to get them! Remember, when I left them, it was about midnight! It is now almost 2 A.M. and the bars are all closing!

As luck would have it, because it was closing time, the traffic in Lower Greenville was like a parking lot! I wish you could have seen the sight I saw when I finally pulled up to get the rest of the ladies! There were 9 drunk ladies, sitting on the curb, dressed in their party clothes looking a bit frazzled! As they were getting in the limo, they were all trying to talk at once and asking what took me so long! I then had to relay the whole Mary story to them! It wasn't a pretty story...but looking back, I guess it was better to laugh at it than to cry!

I was thinking on the way back to let them out, as I was listening to their chatter, that bachelor parties end up so different than bachelorette parties do! The guys are all passed out and the girls are back there still laughing and having a good time!

Life is good!

Bachelorette Party-
In the Limo

*W*omen…God certainly made them different than men! And I personally am so very glad that he did! Again, bachelorette parties are as different from bachelor parties as chicken is from grits!
Two characteristics of many bachelorette parties are that most all of them want the moon roof open and they *all* want champagne! One group in particular planned to party in the limo. They wanted to drive around to a number of memorable places in town so they could get out and take pictures. Of course, the longer I drove, the drunker they got! Champagne has a strange effect on a lot of women! What is really fun to watch is that a lot of the women at these bachelorette parties are now married themselves and have gotten out of the habit of going out and partying all weekend and drinking. So, they started to feel the effects of the champagne pretty quickly! Even after an hour or so, the laughter and talking in the back of the limo sounds like a very large chicken house!!

They took a break to stop at a restaurant to eat…and drink! At the restaurant, I believe the drinks got a little varied which just added to the effects of the champagne! Some of them realized they couldn't hold their liquor like they used to! I'm really glad none of them started losing any clothes at that point! After supper…the limo party continued!

While the ladies are catching up with everyone's news, they all have stories to tell and they are all trying to tell them at the same time! The stories they could tell would make a hooker blush….let alone a limo driver! BUT, they sure were having fun!

When midnight came, it was time to head home. They asked that we drive around a little while longer, so I agreed, and that's what we did. The moon roof was still open. I noticed the ladies taking turns laughing and giggling and standing up through the moon roof. After a few minutes, some police officers pulled up next to me with their lights and sirens on and pulled me over. I asked what was wrong. They told me the ladies in the back of the limo were standing up in the moon roof with nothing on!!! I had not realized that! Luckily, they said, 'We're gonna let you go this time…because we kind of enjoyed the show!'

Thanks to Dallas's finest officers, we didn't get a ticket that night, and the ladies and bachelorette had a night to remember….well, I hope they remembered it! I sure did!

Bachelorette Party-Strip Club

I drove lots of ladies around town for bachelorette parties during my 30 years, but this one was one of the most memorable ones. I'm sure you will soon find out just why it stands out in my memory!

As usual, when I picked up the bridal party, all of the ladies were very excited to get out and party and "let their hair down" for a while. They began by going to a restaurant for a good meal and then they decided they wanted to go to some clubs so they could dance. As you can imagine, drinking was part of the letting their hair down which in turn, loosened them up for the dancing! After a couple of hours of letting their hair get longer and them getting looser, they decided they wanted to go to a strip club! The only catch to that idea is that women are not allowed unaccompanied in a Gentlemen's Strip Club! Since they were so loose with long hair, that did not deter them!

Suddenly I had eight or nine *dates*! I became the *token* male! We got in the club and all the ladies got seated. They seemed to be enjoying watching the girls dance. They had gotten some dollar bills as they entered so they too could pay the dancers for *table dances*, etc. Everyone was drinking and having themselves a good time!

Finally, all of the girls were ready to leave…except the one who was paying for everything! She had never been to a men's club and she was enjoying herself! Since I could not leave to take them home and leave her there alone without a male companion, I called one of my other limo drivers to come take the larger group home so I could stay with her.

By the time the other ladies left, we'll call the one that stayed, Susan, had gotten very chatty with several of the dancers! They started inviting Susan to go back to their hotel with them after the show! I personally began to feel very uncomfortable with the way things were progressing! However, Susan, in her drunken state, seemed to think it was a *great idea!* After all, she had never done anything like this before! At closing time, the dancers began to insist that Susan go in their car with them to their hotel! I could see so many ways that things could go wrong with that scenario! I spoke up and told them that I was going to drive Susan in the limo. Finally, we all headed out to the hotel.

I still had a knot in the pit of my stomach when we arrived at the hotel because things just didn't feel right. The dancers got out and came to the limo to wait for Susan. By the time they got there, I realized Susan had passed out in the back. I told the dancers that she was fixing her hair and I would bring her up to the room when she got finished. They gave me the room number and went upstairs. As soon as they left, I jumped in the limo and headed for Susan's house!

I knew where I had picked her up from, so I just took her home. I managed to wake her up, which wasn't an easy task to wake up a drunk person. I then got her keys and helped her into her house and then to her bed. Once I got her on her bed, I left and left her keys on her dresser.

Susan called me the next morning from her office apologizing profusely for her behavior the night before! I told her what I have told so many people before*: "Sometimes, what happens in the limo stays in the limo!"*

This is the first time I have told this story after all of these years. And I tell it now because it was a very unique one! By the way…the names have been changed to protect the innocent! (smile)

Bachelorette Party-
Stripper Pole

When you get a bunch of women together, you can never really know what is going to happen. But, if there is champagne, loud music, flashing lights, lots of laughter, and...women, there's going to be some fun!

This particular party took place in one of my party buses! The party bus is/was a rolling private party complete with a bar, flashing lights, a music system, comfy seats...and a stripper pole! Or, some people might just call it a "ceiling support system," but I think calling it a "stripper pole" really fits it better!

We started the night by stopping at a couple of restaurants for a good meal and then for dessert. Afterwards, they wanted to stop at a couple of clubs to dance and then for a quick trip to Le Bare, which is a club for ladies that has male dancers, similar to the dancers at the gentlemen's clubs.

Leaving Le Bare, the party continued to rock along as the champagne continued to flow! Finally, one of the ladies "discovered" the stripper pole! Once she finished with her pole dance, every other woman in the party had to take their turn! That was when the party *really* got started! It started getting so good (the best I could see in the rearview mirror while I was driving) that they started taking pictures!

What was really interesting was the difference of the dances and poses from one generational group to the next! The 20 somethings had different poses versus the 30 and 40 somethings! I believe there were even some 50 somethings in the pole dancing group! ALL of those ladies did have fun!! I hated to see the night end and I'm sure they did as well!

When we got back to their starting place, as everyone was getting off the bus, they wanted to have a group picture, with me included! I always loved it when the people that I got to drive around wanted to include me in their group pictures! Of course, there were also lots of hugs, which I always enjoyed too and along with the hugs, I also got TIPS! YES, I actually got paid to have this much fun!

I think you can see by now why this was such an amazing business that I was so blessed to be a part of!

Barry Corbin
Official Voice of 99.5
The Wolf Radio

*A*nother one of the amazing people I got to take places frequently was actor, Barry Corbin. He appeared in movies, and television programs that included Walker, Texas Ranger that starred Chuck Norris and Northern Exposure where he played the part of businessman, Maurice Minnifield, for which he was nominated for two Primetime Emmys.

Although he had been an actor for many years, when I met him, he had become the "official voice" of 99.5 The Wolf Radio Station. I would pick him up about once a month at his ranch in Ft. Worth and take him to the Wolf studio to record one-liners for their advertising and promotional spots.

He was absolutely amazing when it came to recording these spots. Most people would have had to practice a few times to get each one right, but not Barry Corbin! He got every one of them right...the very first time! He would record 3 or 4 pages of the one-liners in a very short time! I loved being able to sit and watch him sail through his recordings! It was a thing of beauty!

What was just as amazing was taking him to places to record commercials. Again, he would nail it the first time. The places we would go for him to do the recordings would have an hour or so set aside for him to record, but he would be finished in 15 or 20 minutes! He was truly a master at those types of things!

I also got to take him to some of the Cowtown events in downtown Ft. Worth. There would usually be a booth set up for him to sign autographs and talk to the people who were in town for whatever event that was being celebrated there! He always loved to talk to the people and he was proud to tell them that he was a cowboy!

Another event that was near and dear to Barry's heart that I got to take him to on several occasions was to the North Park Mall in Dallas where he would be the Grand Marshal to kick off the Susan G. Komen – Walk for the Cure for Cancer! On the way over there he would practice saying, "On your mark, get set, go!" On the way back to his ranch he would always tell me how much it meant to him to get to participate in this event to fight cancer!

One of my favorite things was getting to see his 15-acre ranch. It was in a cul-de-sac at the basin of the Trinity River. His horses got to run free all around that beautiful area. He told me that he rode his horse as often as he had time.

In addition to getting to take him to some of his business commitments, I was also privileged to take him and his daughter and other family members on some outings as well!

Britney Spears

The first time I got to drive Britney Spears was when she was just coming into her fame and popularity! I remember picking her and her group up at the hotel and taking them to the venue where she was going to perform. She was so young and innocent looking. She seemed like nothing but a child.

Another time later that she came back to Dallas, I didn't drive her, but because I worked with all of the radio stations in Dallas, I was able to take my granddaughter, Kaitlyn, backstage to meet her. We chatted for a while, had pictures taken with her, got her autograph, and then she gave Kaitlyn a teddy bear! Before the concert started, a couple of the stage hands took two chairs out front and put them in front of the front row for us to sit to watch the concert. Those were the best seats in the house!

A few minutes after the concert had started, a fellow behind me tapped me on the shoulder. I turned around and he asked me how did we get the tickets for those seats. He said that he and his girlfriend had flown in on a private jet from Florida and had purchased front row seats, but we were sitting in front of them. His girlfriend was upset. Kaitlyn heard what was going on and offered for us to swap seats with them! We did and the young woman finally started really enjoying the concert! As a matter of fact, they had brought a professional photographer along with them to take pictures!

After the concert, the man asked me if I had a business card and told me he would send me pictures of the concert! I gave him my card, but I did not really expect to get any pictures! About a month later, to my surprise, I received about 100 color photos of the concert for Kaitlyn and myself! Just that simple act of kindness of letting them have the front row seat that they had so greatly desired, ended up blessing us with a ton of memories that we got to keep as well!

You never go wrong by doing right!

I was so blessed to live the life in the limo business that I did!

Cheap Trick

As I have said quite a few times I was extremely blessed to be able to work with all of the 26 radio stations in the Dallas/Ft. Worth area and this is just another story of one of those amazing events I was able to experience!

One of my friends from one of the radio stations asked me if I wanted to go meet the band, Cheap Trick, at Billie Bob's. Of course, I couldn't and wouldn't say no to an opportunity like that. Besides, at that time, I had not been to Billie Bob's, which was becoming one of the places to "see and be seen" at in Ft. Worth!

When we arrived at Billie Bob's, I was struck by how large it was! One of the first things we did was to go find the mechanical bull we had been hearing about! Well, we found it; I rode it; and I got ***thrown off of it*** just about as quickly as I got on it! That was a quick lesson learned...**I'm not a bull rider**... and ***I don't want to be a bull rider***!!

The dance floor was huge! It was a good thing that it was huge because the night we were there, the place was packed! At times there was hardly enough room to shake your booty!

The concert area was large as well! Because of our status, we had front row seats, so it was easy to find them. That was enough to make us feel special right there! By the time we found our seats, it was a couple of hours before Cheap Trick was to perform. It was time to go back and meet the band!

It has been my observation that most of the performers that I have met have been down to earth, kind, generous people. The difference between them and me was that they had a talent that they were blessed enough to get to share with the world and they were at the right place at the right time to step into their destiny. Cheap Trick was no exception. They were just 'good old boys' who were just great guys to get to hang out with. Before it was time for them to go on stage to perform, they autographed a picture for me...and gave me a guitar!

By the time they got on stage, we had gotten back to our front row seats. As the concert got started, they said hello to George in the audience! Man... it has been good to be me!!

I kept the guitar on my wall for years, even though I had no idea how to play it. It was just a super piece of memorabilia that no one else in the world had, but me...Limo George!

Cheaters TV Show

I have done some really interesting things during my years in the limo business. However, one of the things that I look back on with some fond and funny memories as well as some doubts as to why I did it was the 5 years I worked with the Cheaters TV Show!

In case you can't figure out what the show was about from looking at the name of it, it was about people who believed their loved ones were being unfaithful or...cheating on them! As you can imagine, the creators of the show had detectives on staff that would "tail" the people who were suspected of cheating and when and if they were actually caught cheating, the host of the show, Tommy, myself (as security), and the camera crew would accompany the person to catch the cheater in the act!

Most of the time, the reactions were pretty funny, but one time in particular, it was downright scary!! Let's just call the lady that thought her husband was cheating on her, Jasmine. And, let's call her maybe cheating husband, Larry. Well, like most wives, Jasmine just had that itchy feeling that something was going on with Larry. Maybe he wasn't scratching her itch...or something like that. But Jasmine wanted answers.

The detectives started following Mr. Larry. Being the kind, helpful, brother-in-law that he was, every night he would pick up his sweet little sister-in-law, Jolanda, from work since Jasmine was at work.

The only problem was that before he took sweet little Jolanda home, he would have to swing by Wal-Mart (actually that would be the dark spot behind the warehouse out back of Wal-Mart) to visit with Jolanda before he took her home! Jolanda must have really hated to go home so early since they had to delay going home most every night!

Once the cheating pattern was established, the producers contacted Jasmine for the confrontation! (By the way, I was along for security.) Since they knew what the usual time schedule was, they had me to pick up Jasmine and wait away from the rendezvous place until the cheaters were in place! The producers gave them plenty of time to get their little meeting started. Once they gave the signal, the camera crew, the host, and the limo (me) with Jasmine swooped in for the gotcha moment! *When the camera lights hit Larry's car, all we could see was his naked behind through the windshield!!* Jasmine jumped out of the limo screaming and crying and having a wall-eyed fit on Larry! Larry had NO IDEA WHAT JUST HAPPENED!! He was trying to get his clothes on amidst all the ruckus! Sweet little sister Jolanda was crying and trying to get her clothes on…and it was some kind of a mess!! But hey, the show must go on…after all, that's why it was called *Cheaters*!!

After she finished with most of her fit, Jasmine wanted to go home and Tommy, the host, had someone drive her there. About the time they left with her…the Dallas Police came storming in with lights and sirens! There were about 5 or 6 police cars and about 10 of Dallas's finest jumping out of their cars with guns drawn and shining flashlights on all of us trying to determine what was going on! I thought I had been afraid before in my life, but I had never been as afraid as I was having the police pointing their guns and flashlights at me in the middle of the night, in a dark place behind a warehouse! What made the situation look even worse was that the majority of us (producers, camera crew, the host, and me) were all white and the cheaters were both black. The police were reading something racial ALL OVER THIS THING!!

Finally, one of the officers asked who was in charge and Tommy, the show's host, spoke up and explained what was going on. About half way through the explanation, most of the officers had lowered their weapons and turned off their flashlights! We all began to take a sigh of relief, except for Larry and Jolanda, who of course still had to face the music with Jasmine when they got home!! I would not have wanted to be in either of their shoes for their boots!! I can only imagine that the next TV show this saga turned up in was probably Divorce Court!

I worked with the Cheaters TV Show for 5 years, but I think this one was the scariest one for me considering being held at gunpoint for a while! Your life does really flash before your eyes...!

Country Music Awards- CBS Dallas

*B*rian Purtitt, who was the General Manager of the CBS Radio Stations in Dallas, was a great friend and someone who always felt comfortable having me to drive his most "valuable" people around Dallas. When the CMA Awards were being held in Dallas, Brian called me to carry one of the New York CEO's and his wife and daughter around for the time they were in town for the award show! I knew from the start that this was going to be a fun assignment!

Of course, the CEO was busy with things pertaining to the award show, and that left his wife and daughter with nothing to do…except…hang out with me…and shop! I know, most men don't like to shop, but with as many people as I dealt with that were from out of town that wanted to see what Dallas was like, I had to find the BEST shopping places! Eventually, I actually enjoyed walking around with the ladies and I frequently got to share my opinion about some of their purchases! I found I had taste I never knew I had!

We went to the malls, to different shopping areas, and restaurants and to just some interesting places around town. I also got to go with them to what was called Radio Row where a lot of the celebrities that were in town for the show would gather to interview on air with the different radio hosts. The booths were set up in a line and you could just walk down the line and watch different stars interviewing and even some of them doing an impromptu performance! It was really a neat experience!

During the days that were leading up to the show, different groups would put on performances and anyone that was around could just walk in and watch the show! Since I am a huge country music fan, that was an exceptionally fun time for me! There were also quite a few opportunities to have your pictures taken with the stars! *It was really good to be me! And I got paid to do this!*

Since I had become friends with the CEO's wife and daughter and they had front row seats at the award show, his wife would send me videos of the live performances! That was a cool way to see the show!

Brian would also call me up some time and ask me to pick up someone at the airport and just show them around Dallas. These would be people they were thinking about hiring and they wanted them to get a feel for the Dallas area! So, who better to show them Dallas, but Limo George! I think I should have been an AMBASSADOR FOR DALLAS! I think I would still be a great Ambassador because I LOVE DALLAS!!

THANKS AGAIN, BRIAN PURTITT!

Corpus Christi-105.3 The Fan

orking with the 26 radio stations in the Dallas/Ft. Worth area was always interesting! One fun time comes to mind about a trip I got to take a group of sales people and on-air personalities to the beach at Corpus Christi, Texas. Matt, who was the program director, contacted me about taking the group down there in one of the party buses. He said a friend had a place that could accommodate about 15 people and they were ready for a trip!

All of the arrangements were made, and everyone was gathering at the party bus, ready and excited to get on the road to the beach! To my surprise, they had the largest cooler I had ever seen full of ice and beer ready for the trip! It was so big that we couldn't get it in the front door of the bus, we had to put it in the back door. As luck would have it, just as we pulled off, the cooler turned over and dumped beer and ice all over the bus and the door jarred open and it spilled out on the pavement as well! It took a while to clean up all the beer! Of course, no one was concerned about the ice!

It is approximately 410 miles from Dallas to Corpus Christi, which makes for a long trip. However, when you have a bunch of women drinking beer on a long trip, it requires a *lot* of bathroom breaks! By the time we finally reached our destination, we were 2 to 3 hours *late!* I was exhausted!! Everyone crawled into their bunks and fell fast asleep!

The next morning, everyone, still kind of jet lagged, got up; fixed breakfast; then loaded the bus to head to the beach! At the beach, as they were exiting the bus, we agreed to meet back at the bus in 4 hours to go get lunch. Four hours later, as expected it was like pulling teeth to get everyone gathered back in the bus. There are always a few stragglers to deal with! A nice dinner wrapped up a good day at the beach and then everyone went back to the condo and settled in for the night.

Sunday morning, we all loaded back into the party bus for the multi-hour trip back to Dallas. There wasn't as much drinking and partying on the way back home. Unfortunately, about half way home the bus starts overheating and the air conditioning goes out! Some people were sunburned and that made the heat even more unbearable! We finally stopped for gas…and before we could all get back into the bus, the guy I had hired to drive us…just up and *quit!* Who quits a job 200 miles away from home? We were in the middle of nowhere, in Texas, in the heat of summer! I don't know how he even got home!

Before too long, we got to Waco and the engine just quit! Luckily, we were stopped at a gas station! But the bad news is that the engine was completely dead! I called my office in Dallas to have them send another party bus to pick us up and take us home! We knew it was going to be at least another 3 to 3 ½ hours before they could get there, so I had to think of something to occupy our time!

Since we were at a gas station, I decided the scratch off tickets may be the answer to some fun! I bought a handful of scratch off tickets and went back to the bus. We decided to divide up into teams and play a tournament of quarters. To play quarters, you draw a line in the sand and each team takes turns tossing a quarter toward the line to see which quarter lands closest to the line! Everyone was thrilled to get started playing to take their minds off of our current dilemma! With each toss, the emcee (me) would yell, "This toss is for $1,000,000!" The entire group really started getting into the game with a lot of gusto!! As the teams dwindled, the cash amount was going…*up!* We were having so much fun that we soon forgot that we were actually stranded in Waco, Texas, in sweltering heat, late on a Sunday afternoon!

After about 3 hours, the other bus arrived! We were finally going to get in out of the heat and finish our trip! But…wait…no one paid attention to the new bus arriving! They were not ready to leave. ***They wanted to finish the game!*** So, we finished the game! The best I remember, the scratch off tickets did not yield any large winners, but the challenge of the game was worth it all!

The trip to Corpus Christi ended about 2 o'clock in the morning on that Monday. That was much later than we had planned, but the stop in Waco had turned into the highlight of the whole trip! And it was an absolute fluke!

To commemorate the trip, Matt, the program director, had T-shirts made for everyone that read, "**1st Annual Tournament of Quarters**"!

Who knew that a broken-down bus would yield the best part of a trip to the beach?

The Dallas Desperados
The Dallas Cowboys
Arena Football Team

I had the privilege of working with the Dallas Cowboys on many occasions and one season I particularly enjoyed was working with their Arena Football Team, the Dallas Desperados.

Jerry Jones began the franchise team in 2002 with his son-in-law, Shy Anderson, as the COO of the team and took care of the day to day operations. The Desperados played in the Eastern Division of the Arena League from 2002 until the franchise was dissolved in 2008.

We usually would pick them up 2 to 3 times per week and take them from one practice area to the other. Nothing was ever on a regular basis with them. We would just get a call from Coach Willis telling us where to pick them up, where to take them, and when to take them back.

They really had a lot of good players on the team. The team was considered a powerhouse in the Eastern Division of Arena Football, but did not fare nearly as well when they were moved to the Southern Division.

The team was disbanded in 2008, but during the time I was working with them, I met a lot of fine young men, and Coach Willis was one of the nicest men I could ever have hoped to work with!

Dallas Summer Musicals- The Stars

I had a contract to carry the stars of the Dallas Summer Musicals around for their publicity meetings. Those were always interesting. A typical day would begin with them making the morning news show rounds between Channel 4 and Channel 8. What was always a fun part of picking the stars up for the morning meetings was that the people that made the schedule would typically check with the stars to see what they would like to drink in the limo on the way to the TV station. Of course, that meant that I would have to be the one that would have to stop to at Starbucks (the vendor of choice) and pick up their custom designed coffee delicacies! The main problem was that they all had so many words in the description that I was never quite sure if they came out exactly like they wanted them or not! They all began like latte grande mocha caramel drizzle something or other! Most of them didn't complain, which probably wouldn't have mattered much anyway since we were usually on a very tight time schedule once I picked them up!

I enjoyed the television interviews for the morning shows since I got to stand behind the cameras and watch from an angle most people don't get to see from. The interviews would usually include the star either singing a song from the upcoming production or if there was more than one of the stars there, they might perform a brief scene from the show. Either way, I enjoyed listening and watching the performances.

Another thing I found interesting were the stars I chauffeured from California who would almost always get excited when they would see an In-and-Out Burger along the way on our trip. After a few of them mentioning the place, I decided I would try it. After all of their excitement about the In-And-Out Burger, it must be something outstanding! However, I tried it…and I quickly decided, I much prefer my Whataburger to the In-And-Out Burger… any day!!

Another fun outing where I got to take the stars of the Dallas Summer Musical was to one of the Texas Rangers baseball games. They were treated like VIPs! We were allowed to park in front of the stadium and a golf cart picked them (us) up and took them down to the ground level to the dugout area. One of the stars was to sing the National Anthem. It was very special to be able to watch them walk out on the field in front of thousands of people and sing the National Anthem! I am very patriotic and that was an incredible experience for me! After they sang, we were taken up to one of the VIP suites to watch the game. There was a great buffet waiting with all kinds of great food and drinks to enjoy during the game. A little before time for the game to be over, we were ushered back down to the limo to avoid the crowd. It had really been a fun and exciting day for them…as well as for me! Have I mentioned lately that I loved my job?

The 4th of July one year provided another fantastic opportunity with the Dallas Summer Musical stars. They were invited to watch the fireworks from the press box of the Cotton Bowl. We arrived just before dark and made our way to the top of the stadium to the press box. To our surprise, they had a huge buffet prepared for us to enjoy. About 8:30 they were ready to begin the fireworks. Words cannot describe how beautiful the view was being that close to the fireworks. What was even more wonderful was that there were 7 more firework shows going on around Dallas at the same time and we could see the fireworks bursting in the sky from all of them. The views were absolutely incredible! Again, I loved my job!

Deer Park - Christmas Light Tour #1
Sure, Blame the Driver!

During the holiday season, particularly Christmas, people love to plan events that involve riding in limos, mostly because they can travel in groups and still have fun! Also, primarily because they can drink like fish and not have to worry about getting a ticket! Of course, the drinking thing is actually a public service thing and actually saves lives during that happy time of the year which is *always a plus!!* It is also very good for the limo business!

Christmas light tours are always big crowd pleasers during the holidays! An interesting fact about most light tours is that the beverage of choice is… you guessed it…champagne! That bubbly drink is the number 1 choice for many festive occasions and some not so festive occasions. This particular light tour was no exception!

Deer Park Subdivision in Plano, Texas, has always been a favorite place for Christmas light tours because of its rather unique layout. There are lots of cul-de-sacs, which were difficult for limos to maneuver in, but the beauty of the area is well worth the extra trouble!

We had two limos to accommodate one group on this night. About half way through the neighborhood, most people were ready for us to stop and let them get out and stretch their legs and walk around a bit. They then decided that half of each limo group would swap limos so they could visit with the entire group. Some mentioned the need to use the restroom, but *unfortunately, no one opened their homes for that service!* After about 10 minutes, everyone reloaded and off we went to finish the tour!

The second half of the tour took about another hour and then we headed back to Dallas to wrap up the night. Just as we arrived back at the starting point where all of their cars were parked, a taxi cab drove up. To everyone's surprise, an irate woman got out of the cab! We were all shocked at her behavior! **Imagine _my_ surprise when I realized this woman was _mad at me_**! She was incensed that I had gone off and left her!! It seemed that during the leg-stretching break, she needed to use the bathroom, so she sneaked off and went up in the bushes beside someone's house to pee. Unfortunately for her, she didn't tell anyone, _not even her husband!_ She insisted that I should have counted the people before we left! (**_Really, these were adults!_**)

At this point her husband made his way up to her asking where she had been! Then, she became irate with _him!_

Seeing my opportunity to leave, while she was chewing him out, I motioned to the other driver to go! We quickly got in the limos...and wished them all a Merry Christmas...and to All a Good Night!!

Dick Clark
"America's Oldest Teenager"

I had many wonderful experiences in my career driving limos, but I have to say being able to chauffeur Dick Clark and his wife, Kari, to the grand opening of the newest American Bandstand Diner was probably close to the top of the list!

I got a call one day from Dick Clark Productions asking if I would be able to pick up Dick Clark and his wife and take them to the grand opening of his new restaurant. Since he was my idol, I would have happily dropped anything I had planned for that day to accept the assignment, which I did! I was given the time and date instructions for picking them up at the airport. However, the last part of the instructions I found to be a little bit unusual! The representative stated that they did not like to ride in fancy cars, so they had already rented a car at the airport and I just needed to go to the car rental place and pick it up. (Strange, really strange, after all, *I did own a limo company!*) Nonetheless, I did comply!

When I arrived at the car rental, there was a rather plain looking Cadillac sitting out front as if it were waiting to be picked up. I identified myself and told the attendant I was probably supposed to pick up that Cadillac out there for Dick Clark Productions (feeling kind of important). The attendant looked up from his paperwork with what appeared to be a bit of a smirk and said, "No sir, you are picking up that little Ford Escort over there."

An Escort, really...Limo George was supposed to drive his IDOL, Dick Clark, in an Escort?! I swallowed my pride (what was left of it), took the keys, and picked up the ESCORT!

Dick and Kari Clark were waiting when I got to the gate to pick them up. When I took them out to the Escort they both smiled as they saw the puzzled look on my face!

As I drove them to the diner, I couldn't help but listen to them talking among themselves and it really touched my heart that even though he was my idol and probably the idol of many thousands of other people, he was just an ordinary man. They were just an ordinary couple. They were discussing what they needed to do when they got home, like taking out the trash and walking the dog! I didn't know that celebrities did normal things like that! I was impressed!

At the American Bandstand Diner, it was amazing to watch Dick Clark. He blended in with the crowd. He went to each table and talked with everyone, signing autographs, and having photos taken. There was nothing stuffy or pretentious about him or his wife. I was sitting in the back of the room taking in the actions of my idol!

While I was sitting there watching him, I starting calling some of my friends to tell them who I was driving that day! Most all of them wanted me to see if I could get an autograph for them! So, I started making my autograph list! After a couple of hours, Mr. Clark wandered to where I was sitting and asked what I was doing. I laughed and told him I was telling my friends who I was driving that day and making a list of those who wanted an autograph. To my surprise, he said, "Come on, George, let's go up to the front and get some T-shirts!" He took me up front and got two or three handfuls of T-shirts and took them to the back and went down my autograph list and autographed each one to my family and friends! Needless to say, that is what everyone got for Christmas that year!!

As we drove back to the airport that evening, I couldn't help but smile as I listened to them talk between themselves. It was the sweet, everyday talk between two people who loved each other and lived normal everyday lives. Dick was to empty the garbage cans from around the house and then take the garbage out. Kari was to feed the dog and then take him/her for a walk. Just everyday living was what they couldn't wait to get home to, not some loud, fancy, star-studded life.

I truly hated for the day to end because even though he had been an idol of mine because of what I had seen of him on TV, he was more of an idol now because I saw what sweet, nice, kind, regular people he and his wife were!

I must admit, the least favorite part of that day was driving a Ford Escort! I'm a big man, used to driving a big, luxury car...and an Escort isn't big or luxury!

Eddie Robinson
NCAA Coach of the Year

Celebrities are literally everywhere! I was privileged to take the winningest college football coach in history and his lovely wife, Doris, to an awards event in his honor! He was Eddie Robinson, head coach of Grambling University.

His accomplishments are almost too many to mention other than to say that he was considered to be the most successful college football coach in FCS history and the third most victorious in college football history.

He and Doris were so cute in the back of the limo. I heard her reminding him what to say and what not to say. She was adjusting his tie and his jacket. I believe she was visibly more nervous than he was! After a little more sweet talk, I heard Eddie tell Doris he wanted to pray. He prayed the sweetest prayer over his speech, the ceremony, the guests, the hosts, and everyone that was going to be there! It was one of the most heartfelt prayers I believe I have ever heard. It wasn't long before we arrived at the venue.

When I helped Eddie and Doris out of the limo, she looked at him with such love and pride in her eyes! She adjusted his tie one more time, he gave her a little kiss, and then they walked into the building! The night could officially begin. The honoree had arrived.

Eddie was being honored by the NCAA. That honor was designed for the college coach whose team excels on the field, in the classroom, and in the community.

Because of everything he did for Grambling University, they named their football stadium the Eddie Robinson Stadium in 1983. They also named a street on the campus after him. While he was coaching at Grambling, his record was 408 wins – 165 losses – and 15 ties.

The trip back to their hotel was just as sweet as the trip to the event. Just watching the two of them talking and giggling made me appreciate the great man who was being celebrated that night, as well as the wonderful woman who might just have been "the wind beneath his wings!" We'll probably never know.

Drag Me to San Angelo...

*W*hen you own a limo business, you really have to be a very trusting soul! I didn't have any idea how trusting you had to be when I got into this business, but I learned pretty quickly that you probably should question more of the details when you are being asked to drive a great distance that involves spending the night! And, you also really need to question exactly what it is that you are going to be doing once you drive that long distance if your participation is going to be required! ***I learned the hard way that it can be pretty scary when you don't ask!!***

I had a client who commissioned me to take her and two other ladies to San Angelo, Texas, which is about 258 miles from Dallas. We left on Friday afternoon and got there late that evening. On Saturday morning we all enjoyed shopping in the little shops in San Angelo and soaking up the local culture! It was during this time that the ladies informed me that "we" were to judge a beauty pageant that evening and by "we," it meant I was included as well! I thought to myself...*judging a beauty pageant might be a fun thing to do on a Saturday evening! There's nothing wrong with looking at pretty women...and picking the prettiest and most talented one...was there?*

The time finally came for us to go to the event! The ladies already had packed and were ready to put everything in the limo when I got there to pick them up. So, we would be ready to leave for Dallas when the pageant was over! ***At that very moment...we had no idea how very "ready" we would be to head out for Dallas!!***

As we entered the gymnasium, it was *full* to the rafters! I don't think there was a single seat left! I remembered thinking, *wow, this must really be a popular event around here!* (I HAD NO IDEA!)

The sponsors recognized my clients and ushered us to a room where they began giving us the instructions for the criteria we were to use in judging the contestants! (This judging thing was new to me!) **Then the shocker came…** *.all of the contestants were transgender…they were men dressed like women!* I believe the women were as shocked as I was! We were instructed that we were not to smile or laugh at any of the contestants, we were always to keep on our judge faces! (I truly believe the three ladies with me were as surprised as I was!)

Let the contest begin!! The contest started promptly at 7:00! I was absolutely amazed! The majority of the contestants were *beautiful* and *very talented!* Judging proved to be considerably more difficult than any of us had anticipated when we began! We did finally narrow the field down to the final 4 contestants! They were all 4 pretty much knockouts! *At this point we all noticed a shift in the mood of the crowd!* It appeared half of the crowd was cheering for one of the ladies and the other half was cheering for the other lady! The noise of the crowd started to sound a little rowdy!! Rowdy is not good when you and three ladies are about to light the fuse to cause that rowdy to explode into a run for your life scenario!

So, being smarter than the average bear, the four of us went to the room in the back and selected the winner! Regardless of who the winner was, we knew half of the crowd was not going to be happy! So we wrote the name of the winner on a piece of paper, sealed it in an envelope, and gave it to the emcee to read. *While he was getting back to the stage and building up the anticipation of the crowd, the four of us were heading to the limo and getting out of San Angelo!!*

In a few minutes, the emcee called the ladies to find out where we were, and they told them we were on our way back to Dallas! As I looked in the rear-view mirror, you guessed it, there was a long line of cars in hot pursuit of us! But Limo George knew better than to let them catch us!!

So you can take it to the bank that this limo driver never volunteered to be a judge of anything ever again unless I knew in advance what I was judging!!

F B I-eyiiiiiii

One year, business was a little slow and I needed some money so I decided to sell one of my limos. I had listed it for sale for $25,000.

After about a week, I had a man call me to come see it. He liked it and decided he wanted to buy it, which was great news for me. He asked if he could pay me $20,000 cash and pay the rest of the $5,000 over the period of a year's time. Since I was short on cash, I decided to take his offer. We signed the paperwork and he left with the limo.

About six months later, I got a call from the FBI! To begin the conversation, the FBI agent asked me if I owned this particular limo. I told him that technically I sold the car to this other man and I was holding the note for the balance. Luckily, I had all of the proper paperwork showing the sale to this man.

I, of course, was curious as to what had happened with the man who had bought my limo. So I asked the agent what had happened.

He explained that the FBI had been doing surveillance on this man and what he was using the limo for. On this particular night that they were watching the man and the car, there were about five guys and a number of women out on a night on the town. They had gone to Shreveport to gamble at one of the casinos. The men would go into the casino, gamble and drink for a while and then come back out to "play" with the women. This went on all night. At about daybreak, they all loaded back up in the limo with the women and started back to Dallas.

Shortly after they were headed back to Dallas, the FBI surrounded the car and pulled them over. Once everyone was out, they started searching the car from the back to the front! The trunk of the limo was completely loaded with marijuana, and under the seats on the inside were loaded with bags of cocaine!! When the agents were checking the registration on the car, it still showed me as the owner. Of course, they were convinced that they had caught a *drug king-pin*...named Limo George!!

I eventually had to make a trip to Washington, D.C., to meet with the FBI and prove that I was not associated with the criminal activities of the man that had purchased my limo.

About six months after my trip to Washington, I received another call from an FBI agent letting me know that they had cleared me from the criminal activities and I could come and pick up my vehicle in Shreveport. At this point, I was still concerned that it was just a setup to arrest me!

I got the address in Shreveport and took two of my limo driver friends with me to pick up the car. The address that I was given was in a pretty remote area that made me question again if this was a setup.

I rang the bell on the gate and the gate started opening. A voice came over the speaker and told us to come in. Once inside, we met a man who had the paperwork and keys to the limo. I signed for the car and we left as quickly as possible...just in case they changed their minds!

After we had gotten out of Shreveport about 50 miles, we pulled off at an exit to check out the car! *Everything* in the limo had been stripped out. They had basically left just the shell of the car!

Needless to say, I had to have the entire interior of the limo recreated. Once it was back in usable condition, I put it up for sale again! This time, I made the man who purchased it pay the full amount at the time of the sale! I wasn't going to take a chance on something else happening with this limo.

I jokingly refer to that year as the year that I sold the same car *twice!* The experience was somewhat scary....but the money was definitely worth it!

Fossil Rim Wildlife Center

I never knew from one week to the next what wonderful adventure might be around the next bend! One of my most unusual journeys took me to the Fossil Rim Wildlife Center in Glenn Rose, Texas.

Three families hired me to take them and their children to the wildlife center at Glenn Rose for a day trip to see the animals. What most people, as well as these parents, don't realize is that the tour to see the animals is actually a bumpy, rutty, dirt road! It definitely is not the kind of road that you want to take a stretch limo…but I didn't know that when we started out, but I certainly realized it once we entered Fossil Rim!

We all learned a lot from the trip! Many of the animals there are endangered species, and many of them are just fun and unique animals that most people do not get to see unless they are fortunate enough to either go to a zoo or a place like this.

The speed limit there is about 15 miles per hour for a good reason. As I mentioned, the roads are dirt…full of ruts, and large bumps! While most of my attention was directed towards keeping the limo from bottoming out on the road, I could hear lots of squeals, giggles, and laughs coming from the back of the limo. The most interesting sight was when I looked in the rearview mirror and saw a giraffe sticking its head through the moonroof eating the treats the kids were feeding him! For some reason, at that very moment, I didn't even think about the giraffe slobber that was probably getting on the roof of my car!

There were animals everywhere! According to the information about Fossil Rim, there are over 1,100 animals located over the 1,800-acre compound. I think we saw all of them that day! The children were absolutely thrilled with being able to see so many of these animals up close and being able to feed many of them.

Eventually we came to a place where we could stop and have a picnic. The parents had prepared a great lunch for everyone! The children ate and played and fed the goats and other little animals that were around.

We finally came to the end of the tour and it was time to go home. It had been lots of fun and very interesting, but I was pretty exhausted from dodging all the bumps and ruts in that long dirt road with a stretch limousine, but I still had a two-hour drive to get us back to Dallas.

This trip to Fossil Rim Wildlife Center wasn't one of my usual events, but it was one of my most interesting!

Garland Christmas Lights Tour

Christmas was always one of my favorite times of the year. Each year, a neighborhood in Garland would have a contest decorating for Christmas. The area was a bunch of cul-de-sacs and each individual cul-de-sac would pick a theme for the year. One of the leaders from the neighborhood would call the radio station to let everyone know that the area was ready for the light tours to begin.

After each area was decorated, they would have someone to come and choose the best decorated cul-de-sac for the season. There would always be a party at one of the homes in the winning area. Once the winner was chosen, I would get a call to start bringing people to the area for the Christmas lights tour. To me, the best part about that call was that I always got to attend the parties in each area. The food was always out of this world and the people were some of the best anywhere around! I started getting so popular in this neighborhood that they were almost auctioning me off as to which party would get to have me come to their party! It was lots of fun and it made me feel very special!

One of the cul-de-sacs would always do a theme pertaining to Elvis Presley. My favorite one that they decorated for was Blue Christmas! The whole cul-de-sac was decorated in beautiful blue and white lights and artificial snow all around. The scene looked like something out of a Thomas Kincaid picture. And the best part of all, they had the song, Blue Christmas playing all over the whole area! I wanted to just drive around and around the cul-de-sac looking at the gorgeous sights and listening to...Blue Christmas, by Elvis Presley!

If I was telling you this story in person, I would probably "sing" a few bars of Blue Christmas for you...but lucky you...you just get to read about it! (smile)

Gene Simmons of KISS— Businessman

I had the opportunity to work with Gene Simmons a number of times and it was always a pleasure. This one particular time was no exception, but as usual, it was always interesting and fun…and educational!

I picked Gene up at the airport and was to take him out to the country to visit with some friends. Before we headed out of town he wanted to stop somewhere and pick up some gifts for the children of the family he was going to see.

We stopped at Town East Mall for him to shop. As we were shopping, Gene got lots of stares and whispers. Lots of people at the mall recognized him even though he was trying to be inconspicuous, although it is hard for any man to be inconspicuous when you are about 6 feet 7 inches tall let alone being a celebrity! Once he had finished shopping, all the gifts were loaded up and we headed to the country!

Later that afternoon, I dropped him off at his destination with instructions to pick him back up in the morning.

When I picked him up the next morning, we had to go through Caddo Mills and stopped to get gas. We went inside to get coffee and donuts and the young woman behind the counter recognized Gene! She was absolutely beside herself! Gene was so kind to her, talking and laughing with her like they had been friends forever! He signed autographs and took pictures with her as well. He did the same for other customers that came in, but luckily there weren't many of them that early in the morning or we might have been there all day!

The thing that also impressed me with Gene is that instead of riding in the back of the limo like most celebrities, he chose to ride up front with me!

Can you imagine getting to just sit and talk to Gene Simmons? During our ride back to the city I also learned that he was a very smart businessman. He told me about some of the business dealings he had going on at the time as well as some that he was planning on investing in. He even gave me some business advice. Yes...Gene Simmons gave me...Limo George, business advice! I did take his business advice, and in time, his advice did pay off.

I was always excited to learn that Gene Simmons was going to be my next client! He was definitely one of my favorite people!

Gene Simmons – Fair Park

*B*y working with the radio stations, I often got to work with some of the most famous celebrities that there were at the time. One of my favorite memories was of an opportunity I had to transport Gene Simmons of Kiss to a performance at Fair Park in Dallas.

What made this appointment stand out in my mind was that we had some of the coldest weather that I can ever remember having in Dallas, Texas! *Everything was frozen*! The trees were frozen, the leaves were frozen, doors were frozen, and anything else you could look at or think of were frozen!!

I picked Gene up at his hotel and it was so icy, you had to watch every step! Slipping on the ice at any second was a real possibility! The radio station kept texting Gene asking him if he was going to make it to the venue, and he would ask me if I was sure we were going to make it. I assured him, I was being very careful, but we were going to make it!

Even though I was assuring him, I had my doubts that anyone would show up for the event because of the weather being so severe! However, I was astounded that when I turned the corner to pull up to the venue, **the parking lot was packed!** Even though walking on the ice was treacherous, the people turned out by the thousands to see Gene Simmons!

I guess it really shouldn't have surprised me that so many turned out to see him, but the event was to support our American service members. Gene Simmons is a true patriot and a great American. It was an honor for me to get to know him since I bleed red, white and blue myself!

George Hamilton-Oh Lord...

I did do a number of things with the Dallas Summer Musicals and one of them was to pick up George Hamilton and his co-star every day from their hotel and take them to the music hall.

One thing I learned about George Hamilton was that his tan....probably was not a natural tan. I know you thought he was naturally that dark, but I hate to burst your bubble...but he's not! I'm pretty sure most of that tan was artificial!!

I typically picked him and his co-star up in an SUV instead of the limo which made interacting with them a lot more interesting and fun. Every morning, the three of us would sing the following song all the way from the hotel to the music hall! **"Oh Lord it's hard to be humble when you're perfect in every way! I can't wait to wake up in the morning, I get better looking each day!"** We were all singing to the top of our lungs like we were rock stars...well, two of them were rock stars...but I felt like one singing with them!

It is amazing to me how you can form an opinion about someone and not really know anything about them. However, when you get to know them, your whole opinion changes! I learned that George Hamilton was really a very nice, funny, down to earth person who was truly thankful to be able to make a living doing the things that he loved to do.

When I look back, I felt the same way. I was and am very, very thankful that I was able to be in the limousine business because my life touched the lives of more people than I would have ever met in any other line of business. I would also have to add that I was blessed to have gotten into this business!

Gilley's of Dallas

One of the fun places I always enjoyed going to and taking clients as well as performing groups to was Gilley's of Dallas. Of course, Gilley's was the brainchild of Country and Western legend, Mickey Gilley.

The Dallas location is approximately 92,000 square feet of nothing but fun! I had the privilege of taking a number of bands there to put on concerts. One band I particularly liked taking to Gilley's was the Russ Martin Band. They were my favorites because I felt like part of the band since I got to go backstage and hang out with them before they performed! As a matter of fact, I was the only person Russ would let stay with him in the green room while he was waiting to go on stage! I've got to admit, that made me feel like a *"big wig!"* Even the police that were part of the security there knew who Limo George was and that I was "part of the band!"

Another band I enjoyed taking there was Black and Black. They were the cover band sometimes for the Russ Martin Band. For the most part, the guys (and girls) in the bands that I had the privilege of taking to their performances were just down to earth people who were talented! A lesson I learned very early in my limo career was that the nicer you treated them, the nicer they treated you! You know, that pretty much is true with just about anyone you meet…whether they are rich, or not so rich; talented or not so talented!

It kind of fits right in with that, *"do unto others like you want them to do unto you!"*

The Greenville Avenue Parade
St. Patrick's Day

*I*n Dallas, Texas, there is never a lack of things to do, and certainly the Greenville Avenue Parade that celebrates St. Patrick's Day is always a special occasion! It is the largest St. Patrick's Day parade in the Southwest!

This year I got to work with one of my favorite companies to represent them in the parade. I was working with Terilli's Italian Restaurant. They were one of the premier Italian restaurants in the Dallas area and they were located in the Greenville Avenue area. The restaurant was family owned and they were always looking for ways to interact with the people in the neighborhood.

This parade was sponsored by some non-profit groups to create scholarships for Dallas ISD students. Even though it celebrates St. Patrick's Day, it is more like Mardi Gras in Dallas. If you didn't walk away from the parade with at least a double handful of beads…you had not been at the parade!

For this parade, we had four large boxes of beads to throw to the crowd. There was always in excess of 100,000 people in attendance at any given parade. That's a lot of people, but there was always a lot of fun!

We had a saxophone player sitting in the moonroof opening playing as we inched along in the parade. Waitresses were also hanging out the windows and the moonroof waving, laughing, and tossing beads! Some waitresses were walking along beside the car tossing beads as well. They did such a great job giving away beads, there was not a single strand left!

The atmosphere at the restaurant all day was nothing but party! They were serving their signature Italcho's (Italian Nachos) as well as all of their other amazing signature dishes! Those people knew how to throw a party… for their customers….and the neighborhood!

And, of course…when I am working for a restaurant, I *always* get to eat very well! Have I mentioned lately that I loved my job?!

Horse Races at Grand Prairie

One of the things that I dearly loved was getting to take clients to the horse races at Lone Star Park in Grand Prairie, Texas.

A lot of my clients would have access to the sky boxes at the top of the stands where you could see the entire track at one time which made the races even that much more exciting! When we were in these sky boxes, there was always buffets with great food and drinks that were always incredible! I loved horse racing anyway, but being able to enjoy the races from that vantage point just made the experience that much sweeter!

I had the privilege of being there for the 1st Annual Easter Egg Hunt! I have to admit that was one of the cutest sights I have ever seen watching all of those little children running through the outfield with their Easter bonnets and their Sunday best clothes on looking for Easter eggs! As you would expect, eggs were everywhere, but most of the real little ones didn't understand why they were even running! It was a precious and heart-warming sight that I will always remember...***and I was there for the very first one***!

I had other clients who had access to the second level of suites at Lone Star Park, and those were very nice as well! They also included the great buffets with incredible food and drinks...which I *always* enjoyed!

And even if my clients didn't have access to any of the sky boxes or suites, I had made friends with some of the concierges and they would always find us good seats to be able to have a good meal and watch the races!

I learned a lesson early in life, that if you treat other people like you want to be treated, they will always treat you the same way! I made friends from the lowest to the highest, but I cherish them all the same! There are more truly good people in this world than there are bad! You just tend to hear about the bad ones instead of the good!

Jimmy Buffet
and the Parrot Heads

I had a group of people who I took to the Jimmy Buffet concert on a yearly basis for five or six years. I learned right away that Jimmy Buffet fans are like no other concert fans that I had *ever* seen before!

In case you didn't know, his followers are called Parrot Heads! Many of them actually walk around with fake parrots perched on their shoulders! The first time I saw that phenomena I was shocked to say the least, but hey, each to his own!

On this particular trip with this group to the Jimmy Buffet concert, it started in the morning as most of the Parrot Heads usually chose to do! They would start their tailgating at breakfast and it would last *all day long*! Needless to say, margaritas were the drink of choice! Everybody was full of margaritas by the time for the concert!

The group decided to take their tailgating a little bit further this time! Not only did they have their stuffed parrots, their cutoff shorts, flip flops, and other island paraphernalia, they decided they wanted a TAN! I had to agree, they were all a pasty white!

They found a tanning salon near the concert venue and we were off to get a tan! Little did I know when I turned the limo in the direction of the tanning salon that I, too, would be a glorious 'tan' when I returned!

Everyone was pretty high on margaritas at the tanning salon and they all chose their golden tans for the night. However, they started looking at me through their margarita 'haze' and decided that I was *really* white and that I needed a ***super tan***! So, <u>*they paid for Limo George to get the super tan!*</u>

We returned to the venue with our golden tans and ready for the concert! I have to admit that if you have never been to a Jimmy Buffet concert, you should put it on your bucket list! He puts on a fantastic show and it is very entertaining to listen to his stories!

All seemed well with my 'tan' until the next morning! When I woke up, I started itching all over! Then the bumps started popping up along with the itching! As it turned out, I was allergic to the chemicals in the spray tan! I basically had 1st degree burns all over my face and arms and chest and anywhere else that I had a 'tan'! I was sick for a week! But at least the discomfort didn't start until *after* the concert so that I did get to enjoy being a Parrot Head one more time!

The lesson I learned from that experience was that it isn't necessarily bad to be 'pale', especially after you learn you are allergic to the spray tan chemicals! All I can say is…*never again!!*

Kaitlyn-My Granddaughter

They say that having grandchildren makes having children worth-while! I have to admit that having a granddaughter really set my heart on fire!

She is grown now with two children of her own, but as a little girl, she had her Papa's heart! I couldn't resist sharing a story about her.

From the time she was in elementary school in Highland Park Elementary, I would pick her up every day and take her home. Can you imagine being picked up and riding home every day in a limo? I'm sure everyone thought she was just a poor little rich girl...which she was in one sense!

I continued picking her up from school every day even when she was in high school. One day I picked her up and she was crying. Of course, her tears could open any door with me! It turned out she was crying because she did not have a cell phone! On the way home, I stopped and got her a cell phone! That stopped those tears right away.

The lesson that I learned after getting her the cell phone was that you had to pay, at that time *per text!* They didn't have *unlimited* texts like we do now. You can imagine my utter shock when I got a bill for 30,000 texts!! Yes, that is a 3 and 4 zeros! Believe it or not, she tried to act dumb! However, then she showed me she could text with her eyes closed, behind her back, under her leg, etc!! I was in shock!!! I think we took her phone until we could get unlimited texting! Lesson learned!

By her senior year, she came to me crying again! This time, her momma wouldn't take her to get a prom dress and the prom was coming up! There goes those tears again!! I told her I was on my way to pick her up and we were going prom dress shopping!

I picked her up and she directed me to the boutique she had picked out! When we went inside, they sat me down on a big leather sofa with a television that I could watch while she tried on dresses. In a little while, they bring Kaitlyn out in a dress…I didn't like it, and I said, no, that's not the one. She left and came back in a few more minutes with another one, and it wasn't the one either. Finally, she comes out in a pretty blue dress! I could see that look in her eyes! She said, "Papa, this is my dress!" I knew that was the one she had to have!

I asked if they could have it ready by the next time since it had to have alterations, and of course, they could! Little did I know that the dress cost **$800**! **$800 for a PROM DRESS!** A lot of women don't get to spend that much for their wedding dress, let alone a *prom dress!!* But she had Papa's heart!!

Of course, she looked like an absolute dream in the dress! I did feel sorry for her date to the prom! She was just a little bit spoiled. She wasn't about to ride to the prom in a limo! She had ridden in limos all of her life. Her date had to rent a *Lamborghini* to take her to the prom….that was on top of the corsage and supper!

Besides all of this, she also got to go to more concerts than you can imagine as well as being able to go backstage and even got to go shopping with Brittany Spears!

Like I said, Papa's little girl was just a little bit….spoiled!!

Keep...Sell...Toss!

One night my clients were a group of men from Dallas who were having a bachelor party to celebrate the wedding of a friend of theirs. The party was to begin with a limo ride from Dallas to Shreveport, Louisiana, for them to eat, gamble, and party! I could have *never* imagined what the outcome of that bachelor party would be!

I picked them up at a steakhouse in downtown Dallas where they had already started the festivities of the weekend! There were 9 of them including the groom-to-be, who I will call Bruce. By the time I picked them up at about 10:00 P.M., the groomsmen were laughing and joking about how many raw oysters Bruce had eaten and how many beers and booze he had consumed at the steakhouse! Of course, several of them seemed to be close to his level of intoxication, but that was beside the point! This was a weekend of partying and they had already gotten the party started!

As we began the 3 ½ hour trip from Dallas to Shreveport, I had the window open between myself and the guys in the back to make sure they had everything they wanted or needed. The bar was stocked, the car was cool, and the lights were on...perfect for a party! As they settled into the ride, I closed the window to let them enjoy their privacy for the party! *(You know that what "happens in the limo, stays in the limo'!")*

After about an hour into the ride, one of the guys started banging on the window almost in a panic. He was shouting, "Pull over, pull over, pull over, he's going to puke!" As luck would have it, it was the groom who was sick! I quickly reached for the barf bag in the glove compartment and handed it to the guy through the window. Unfortunately, I had no idea that the barf bag was defective and was not fully sealed at the bottom! Most all of the vile smell-ing puke went into the barf bag....and out the bottom of it all over the carpet, under the bar, and on the shoes of half of the other guys!

From personal experience, most of you know that what happens when you see someone else puke is that it makes *you* want to puke...especially after the ungodly smell hits your nostrils! By the time I could get pulled over, there was a lot of gagging going on! We cleaned up the mess the best we could with what we had available, but the smell was horrendous!

As soon as I could get to the next exit, I pulled into the first gas station I could find! We cleaned it up *again*...the best we could and got all of the cans of air freshener the gas station had...about 10 cans!! It was the most putrid, rotten smell we had ever smelled! It was hard to believe something that smelled this horrific came from a live human being!

The smell was so nasty, I had to stop about every 15 minutes to let the guys get out and take a breath. We continued this stopping process until we finally reached Shreveport. A 3 ½ hour trip took us more like 5 hours.

By the time we reached the hotel, almost all of the groomsmen felt as sick as the groom, just because of the smell! After making sure all of the men were headed to get checked into their rooms, I spoke to the head bellman and asked if he could find someone that time of the night to clean and deodorize the cabin of the limo. He said he would have a friend come and do it immediately. I gave him the keys and went and checked in to the hotel myself.

Later that morning, the guys were able to get up and get out to finally start enjoying their trip to the casinos. They gambled, ate, and played until it was time for us to head back to Dallas.

While they were partying and playing, I decided to check on the limo. I couldn't believe it! Even after the carpet had been shampooed and the seats had all been wiped down and cleaned....the odor was still there!!! This was the odor from *hell!*

When it was time to leave, everyone arrived back at the limo for the trip home! To everyone's shock....the smell was still there!! *What had he eaten to make this smell so impossible to remove?*

The trip home followed the same process the trip to Shreveport had taken...drive 15 minutes, stop and spray the car!

We finally made it back to Dallas. Needless to say, everyone stayed sober for the trip! They wound up giving me an extra $600 to have the limo fumigated!

Having it fumigated *and* cleaned *and* deodorized *did not work!* After about a month, I couldn't stand the smell anymore! I put the limo up for sell. When the customer was on his way to look at it, I used another full can of air freshener to mask the odor....it worked....he bought it!

Finally...the smell was *gone!*

Kid Rock-Cabaret Royale

$\mathcal{I}$ had a contract with Cabaret Royale to take the performers out at different times when they wanted to go somewhere. One afternoon I got a call that they wanted to go out that night and to be there about 9 o'clock to pick them up. They didn't mention where they wanted to go. When I got there, it turned out they wanted to go to the Kid Rock concert at the Bronco Bowl, which used to be a good place to have concerts before it was closed down.

I arrived by 8:30 to be able to leave by 9:00, which by my calculations would still make us late to the concert. I made sure they knew I was there, but, by 10:00, they were still getting dressed! I sent word to them that if they didn't hurry up, they were going to completely miss the concert! Luckily, they soon started trickling out to the lobby!

Finally all ten of them were loaded into the limo and we were off to the concert! We were able to park in the back of the building and they were actually allowed to go into the back room behind the stage. According to my estimation, by the time we got there, only about 10 minutes remained in the concert. I decided that I would just stay in the limo. **I knew that 10 was plenty and _11 would definitely be a crowd_**!!

About an hour and a half later, all of the girls started streaming out of the building. However, instead of the laughing and giggling that they were doing when they went in, they seemed to be arguing and yelling. I could look at their faces and see the "mad" in some of their eyes! Nevertheless, they all got loaded back in the limo and we headed back to the Cabaret! As we are driving along, I hear voices getting louder and louder! Finally, things seem to be out of hand!

I had to pull over into a parking lot to investigate what was going on! When I opened the door, they all were talking at once.

The heated discussion seemed to be over which one of them performed the "best service" for Kid Rock! And by service…you can use your own imagination as to what service they were referring to. I told them I could settle the issue for them right then. They could each perform the service on me and I could tell them which one was the best! However, they all declined my offer!!

They eventually settled down and we proceeded back to the Cabaret. By the time they all got out of the limo and were getting back inside, Kid Rock was pulling up. **I would assume he was there to decide which one, *indeed*, <u>did perform the best service</u>!**

KLUV Wedding

Working with the radio stations, I got to meet some wonderful people that I consider to be lifelong friends. One such relationship that I will always cherish is with Teresa who worked at the KLUV radio station.

Teresa met her "cowboy" on one of the KLUV cruises that the station sponsored. When they decided to get married, they picked a ranch down in Austin, Texas. I got to be the "flower boy" in the limo! All of the flowers for the wedding were coming from Dallas and I was taking them down for the wedding. I can tell you one thing, my limo has never smelled that good since then! It was packed with some beautiful, beautiful flowers for a beautiful bride!

The wedding was held out in what seemed to be the middle of a pasture! It was located up on a hilltop under a large oak tree. In order to get to the area for the wedding, you had to walk through about 2 acres of cow manure. After walking through the cow-patties, you got to sit on bales of hay for the ceremony. When it came time for the ceremony to begin, you could hear the sound of horse hooves headed towards us. On the horses, was the groom and his groomsmen. They rode up, dismounted, and lined up next to the minister.

The next sound you heard was horse hooves and a wagon. The bride and her bridesmaids arrived on the wagon. I must admit, it was a very lovely and touching sight to see Teresa being helped from the wagon in her wedding gown. She was finally getting to marry her "cowboy!"

The ceremony itself was very sweet and joyful! After they said their vows and their I do's, they rode off into the sunset on the wagon with the horse tied to the back. That's how the old West movies used to end! Gorgeous!

Then everyone had to make their way back through the cow patties to where a dance floor had been set up for the party! And, party they did!!

When I left at about 11 o'clock the party was still going strong! I couldn't help but smile when I opened the door to my car and I could still smell the sweet aroma of the flowers that I had transported for my precious friend, the bride!

I was and am so happy that Teresa got to marry her "cowboy," as she always called him! I don't know if it was a match made in heaven, but it sure looked like it from what I could see!

Lesbian Wedding- Almost a Fight

*M*ost of the time I didn't think about it, but on occasions, when you least expect it, the limo business could get a little bit dangerous!

I was hired to take two women out from Rockwall, Texas, to Dallas to get married. The trip out there was pretty uneventful as most trips out of town were. However, I can't say the same was true for the trip back to town!

On the way back to town, they had me to stop and pick up a man. After I picked him up, I started smelling someone smoking in the back of the limo. I opened the window between the back and front of the limo and told him to put the cigarette out that there was no smoking in the limo. He said he would put it out. I closed the window. A few minutes later, I smelled it again. I told them a second time, and I got the same response. When I smelled it a third time, I stopped the limo, got out, and went to the back and told him to get out of the limo! All of the women started begging me not to put him out there! They said they would make sure he didn't smoke again! I got back in the front to finish the trip to their destination.

During the rest of the trip, I started hearing the women in the back talking in the back that they were going to jump me and beat me up when we got to their place for being mean to their friend about smoking! Luckily, they didn't know that I could hear all their plans!

When I pulled up to their destination, I reached over in the seat next to me and picked up my 2-foot-long flashlight before I headed to the back to let them out! When I opened the door with the flashlight raised, I think they changed their minds about an attack! I told them all to stand to the side as they got out. Once they were all out, I closed the door, hurried to the driver's side, jumped in and took off. When I looked in the rearview mirror the group was chasing after the limo!

Who knew that a bunch of women would get ballsy enough to jump a limo driver because he wouldn't let their boy-toy smoke in the limo? Life sometimes is stranger than fiction! I'm just glad I knew how to drive fast!!!

Limo George-Celebrity!

*B*eing a celebrity can be exhausting if you are REALLY popular...**but it can be a lot of fun...*especially when you find out you are one...* and you didn't know you were!** Yep...I didn't realize my "celebrity" status until one night I was driving a group of teenagers to their senior prom!

It started out like a usual prom night pick up. All of the attendees were gathered at one house with lots of parents and pictures being taken! The typical individual couple pictures and the group pictures with all the serious and silly poses!

When all of the pictures were taken and it was time to leave for the prom at Southfork Ranch, all of the kids piled into the limo for "the night of their life" at their senior prom! Before I started driving, I opened the window into the back of the limo to see what kind of music they wanted to listen to for the ride. To my surprise, they picked music that was typically played on The Edge Radio Station in Dallas. I told them I liked that kind of music too and that I got to interact with the Friday morning host on that station. When I said that, you could have almost heard a pin drop. They started looking at each other and whispering back and forth! I asked what was wrong! One of them spoke up and asked me, "Are you Limo George?" I said, "Yes, why?" They immediately started smiling and giggling and started making calls on their cell phones to their parents to let them know that Limo George from The Edge was driving them to the prom!! I had *no* idea that I was *that* popular...especially among this age group (although it was kind of cool)!!

After all the excitement of them learning who I was, they all got really quiet! I asked them why they were being so quiet (most limo rides to the prom are typically loud and rowdy)! One young man spoke up and said they were trying to be polite so I wouldn't talk about them on the radio! Although I tried to reassure them that I wasn't going to do that, they still were acting pretty subdued! I wanted them to have fun, but they still kept the noise and partying to a minimum!

When we arrived at Southfork, they quickly got out and started telling their friends *who* drove them there!

I must admit, I was feeling pretty flattered by all of the attention!!

I left them at the prom to focus on having a great time and make special memories of that night! However, when I returned at the appointed time, there were a lot more students waiting at our pickup spot than just those I had driven there! There were about 50 extra kids there who wanted to see Limo George *and* have their picture taken with me! I was almost speechless....and that is a state I have rarely ever found myself in!!

On the trip home, they were all still being really quiet and polite. I finally had to stop the car and have "***the*" *talk*" with them! I told them I was not going to drive another mile until they started having fun! I said that every one of them had to stand up and stick their head out the moon-roof and whoop and holler before we got back to their house! I think they believed me that time! They finally started acting like normal teenagers in a limo on prom night!!

To my surprise, when I pulled up at the designated house to drop them off, there were lots of parents milling around and having their own party... .waiting to have their pictures taken *with me!!* I think I had more pictures taken of me and with me in that one night than I had had in the previous 10 years!! I think that was one of *my favorite* prom nights!!!

Who knew I was a *celebrity!?*

Make a Wish Foundation

*D*uring my years in the limo business, I had a number of opportunities to work with the Make-A-Wish Foundation in the Dallas, Texas, area. It was a privilege for me to be able to work with this incredible group of people to help make the wishes of some Dallas area children become a reality. Below is some information about this foundation that I believe is worth sharing.

Wishes make life better for kids with critical illnesses. This simple, but powerful belief inspired the founding of Make-A-Wish® and drives everything we do.

Our Mission

Wishes are more than just a nice thing

A wish experience can be a game-changer for a child with a critical illness.

This one belief guides us in everything we do at Make-A-Wish®. It inspires us to grant wishes that change the lives of the kids we serve. It compels us to be creative in exceeding the expectations of every wish kid. It drives us to make our donated resources go as far as possible.

Most of all, it's the founding principle of our vision to grant the wish of every eligible child.

Wishes are more than just a nice thing. And they are far more than gifts, or singular events in time. Wishes impact everyone involved - wish kids, volunteers, donors, sponsors, medical professionals, and communities. The impact varies. For wish kids, just the act of making their wish come true can give them the courage to comply with their medical treatments. Parents might finally feel like they can be optimistic. And still others might realize all they have to offer the world through volunteer work or philanthropy.

Whatever the odds, whatever the obstacles ... wishes find a way to make the world better.

Make-A-Wish- American Airlines

*D*uring my career, I had the privilege and several opportunities to work with the Make-A-Wish Foundation in the Dallas/Ft. Worth area. I can truthfully say, these were some of the most rewarding and heart-rending days of my life. Several stories come to mind about these cherished times!

There was a little boy named Jacob who was suffering from a life-threatening illness (which is one of the criteria for having a Wish granted) and one of his greatest desires was to be one of the people who directs the incoming airplanes into their parking place at the DFW Airport with the "flashlights!" The Make-A-Wish Foundation along with American Airlines, working together were making Jacob's wish become a reality!

On that day, I went to Jacob's home and picked him and several of his family and friends up for his adventure! I was greeted by lots of big smiles and lots of laughter! Jacob was absolutely beaming! Looking at the exuberant kid, you almost couldn't imagine how sick he really was. It is like the old adage that says, *"Laughter is like good medicine!"* It certainly seemed to be working that day!

When we arrived at the Corporate office in Ft. Worth, Texas, that morning, there were literally hundreds of people milling around outside! As I pulled the limo up to the front door and got out, I asked a man standing nearby what was going on. Luckily, it just turned out to be a fire drill! However, when I opened the car door for Jacob and his family to get out, Jacob was visibly very upset! His mother quickly stated that Jacob was very shy and seeing all the people around scared him! So, I let them stay in the limo while I went inside to find the volunteers who were going to be taking us around the office.

As I was entering the front doors Andrew and Christine, our assigned volunteers greeted me and started looking for Jacob. I explained that he was in the limo. They quickly went outside to meet him and his family. By this time, all the people had returned to the building and the excited look lit up Jacob's face again!

Once inside, Andrew and Christine explained to Jacob and his family that our first stop was going to be at the *flight simulator*. Jacob was seated in the Captain's seat and was shown how to *fly* the plane! I had to admit that I almost had as much fun as Jacob did on the simulator! It included every scenario you can imagine that an airplane could encounter. Jacob was even allowed to crash land the plane! I am proud to say that is the only way that I would ever want to be in a *plane crash!*

The next stop for Jacob and his family was a conference room that had been reserved for them where they would be served lunch! After entering the conference room, Jacob was ushered to the head of the table where he was seated. Shortly after being seated, Andrew came in carrying the little uniform that had been made for Jacob so he would be dressed properly for his job! It was an exact duplicate of the uniforms worn by the American Airlines ground crew! The details of the uniform were very accurate, or so it looked to me, and identical to the real thing! He was also given his own set of "flashlights"…. .which aren't actually flashlights! A delicious lunch was served to everyone and the smiles and laughter continued! The excitement in Jacob's eyes was contagious!! It seemed everyone we met for the rest of the day that knew who Jacob was had that same excitement in their eyes! Even though Andrew and Christine were the primary volunteers, many other American Airline employees had helped to make this day unforgettable!

Finally, it was time to head to the airport. Jacob's mother had helped him put on his uniform and he was ready to go! Andrew and Christine accompanied us to the airport to make sure the main event went as planned. The entire entourage was ushered into the area where the ground crew worked. Jacob was introduced to his partner, Juan! Juan had worked in this type of position for 10 years and was well versed in the procedures. They were notified that an American Airlines 747 had just landed and was taxiing to the gate we were at. Juan helped Jacob with his "flashlights" and they got in position! As they assumed the position, in about 10 minutes, the 747 slowly made its approach to the lane for that gate. Jacob was almost beside himself as he and Juan started the signals for the approaching plane. Jacob watched Juan and duplicated what he was doing motioning for the plane to continue to roll forward until it got to just the right place....and then made the "X" motion with crossed arms for the plane to stop! *Job accomplished!* Jacob had helped the plane come to a safe stop at the right spot for the passengers to off-board! Juan got Jacob in a place so he could see the pilot and co-pilot in the window of the cockpit giving him a thumbs up for a job well done!

By the time the day ended, little Jacob was elated and exhausted! Even with his joy and excitement, Jacob fell asleep on the limo ride back home! I didn't get to say good-bye to Jacob at his house, but I had tears in my eyes as they carried his little, sleeping, frail body back into his house, I knew this would be a day he would remember for the rest of his little life....and one I would never forget too!

Make-A-Wish – Domino's Pizza

Some children dream of being astronauts, others dream of being super-stars, and some children just dream of driving an 18 wheeler! That was the wish of a little boy named Eric. Little Eric was suffering with a very debilitating illness that kept him confined to his home most of the time.

Since he had to stay indoors most of the time, he had all kinds of toys to choose from to play with. But, his favorite toy was his Tonka 18 wheeler. Eric used his imagination to drive his 18 wheeler all around town and to places he could imagine across the country! However, pretending to be riding in an 18 wheeler wasn't nearly as much fun as actually riding in one!

Because of his disability, Eric's family submitted a request to Make-A-Wish Foundation for him to be able to have an adventure riding in an 18 wheeler. The Foundation chose to make his wish come true in a somewhat unusual way! Make-A-Wish teamed up with the local Domino's Pizza Franchise in the Dallas area at their warehouse to arrange the details of Eric's day.

When the day finally arrived for Eric's Wish to be granted, I picked up him, his mom and dad, and two sisters bright and early that morning! There were smiles and giggles all over the limo! Seeing such excitement and joy on a child's face like that is a gift of its own! We drove to the Domino's Warehouse where they were met by the MAW (Make-A-Wish) volunteers, Sandy and Amanda, and the Domino's representative, Harry. After introductions were made, everyone was taken to a room where Eric was given his uniform for the day, complete with his name tag which had his position designated as "Domino's Pizza Truck Driver!"

After a brief tour around the warehouse office and warehouse, Eric was introduced to his driver partner for the day, Sam! Sam was a large, burly guy which made Eric look even smaller than he was! He and Sam walking along together looked like a giant and a tiny munchkin! There was also a photographer there that was journaling the event.

Eric was hoisted up into the cab of the 18 wheeler in the passenger's seat and buckled in for the ride of his life! As Sam started the engine, Eric shrieked with excitement! I drove along behind Eric and Sam with the rest of the family and volunteers. As Sam made each stop that day, Eric was allowed to watch him unload at each delivery stop and walk into the Domino's business as the paperwork was signed. Then back into the truck and on to the next stop! Of course, for lunch that day we all had…Domino's Pizza! I'll bet you would have never guessed that one!

At about 4 o'clock, they had made their final stop and we were headed back to the warehouse! By this time, Eric had started winding down a little bit after such an amazing and exhausting day as…..an 18 wheeler truck driver!!

One of the neatest things that happened that day is when we returned to the warehouse office, Eric was again ushered inside. The workers in the office all greeted him and were asking how his day went! Their enthusiasm seemed to revive Eric's spirits again! His little face was still beaming with joy! And then, the manager of the warehouse came out and was introduced to Eric and his family…and he gave Eric a paycheck for his day's work for the company!!

Eric's family, the volunteers, Sandy, Amanda, Harry, Sam, and I enjoyed getting to watch the transformation of a sick little boy into a joyful, animated, and happy – 18 wheeler driver….even if it was just for a day!

Again, the goodness of humanity stepped up to make the heart's desire of a sick child become a reality! Of course, my time was donated as well!

Mary Kay, Inc.

Through the years, working with the Mary Kay Company became a regular, yearly event for me and my company and I loved it! In case you're not familiar with Mary Kay, it is one of the largest cosmetic companies in the world, and most of the people selling their products are beautiful women!!

They had their yearly award ceremonies and sales events and they are huge in Dallas! There are more pink Cadillacs and women dressed in pink than you can stir with a stick! Dallas turns PINK when Mary Kay is in town even though it is the headquarters for the company. These events are enormous!

Luckily for me, I have such a winning smile and lovable personality that I was able to secure the yearly loyalty of a group of those ladies who came to the yearly events. They wouldn't let anyone else drive them around or pick them up but good ol' Limo George! I believe what sealed the deal with that group was the first year I started driving them, after they ate dinner, they all wanted to go dancing. (A well-known fact is that many people, men and women, will try things when they are away from home that they wouldn't necessarily do at home! It's kind of that thing like…what happens in Vegas stays in Vegas, but it works in Dallas too!) Luckily, the place they ate dinner had a live band! Being the suave man that I am, I was privileged to dance with *all* 10 of them! Sometimes it pays to know how to do the two-step!

I would drive them around and show them the sights around Dallas. One of their favorite places was in Las Colinas where there is a metal sculpture of mustangs running in water. A tradition was started that each year we had to visit that sculpture and they would stand in the water and have the picture taken of the group. It was fun to get to see the changes in them over the next five years! During those years, they all continued to grow their business and some became quite wealthy!

At the Mary Kay yearly event, they had their reward night. Because of the tremendous number of women who attended these events, they had 4 day cycles. Each group had 4 days' worth of activities that would culminate in what I called "prom night." They actually called it "rewards night." All of the ladies would dress up in their beautiful formal gowns with all of their jewelry in all of their splendor for their special night! When I picked them up in the limo, the first one in was the last one out! On one occasion, this caused a unique problem.

The first young lady I helped into the limo was typically a very quiet, shy one. As required, she scooted all the way around the seat so the rest of the ladies could be seated! Of course, that meant the first one in was the last one out! Being the gentleman I was, I stood by the limo and held each lady's hand as they exited. It finally came time for the last one to slide around and get out, as I held out my hand to assist her, much to my surprise, her dress (because of all of the sliding on the limo seat) had slid up and up and up until it revealed… .she didn't have on any underwear….none!! There it was…in black and white…or whatever the color was! I feel certain the expression on my face and the color it turned probably said it all! However, very graciously, and with a smile, she laughed and said, *"George, did you see my tonsils?"* That quiet, shy woman turned a very awkward moment into a good laugh!

Because of my popularity with the groups of Mary Kay ladies, on their rewards nights, I might have three or four groups of ladies to transport back and forth to the event. Taking them wasn't much of a problem. I would just take one group, turn around, return to the hotel, pick up the next group, deliver them and repeat until all of my groups were delivered. It was a little more difficult at the end of the night. They were all ready to go back to the hotel at the same time. Since they only wanted me to take them, we just arranged for *my ladies* to gather under a certain tree until I was able to pick them up! It was such a wonderful experience getting to see these groups of incredible ladies each year and hearing about the progress they had made during the year and what rewards they were getting for their hard work!

Another interesting part about my Mary Kay ladies was that I always had to take two limos to pick them up at the airport and to take them back to the airport! One limo carried the ladies, the second limo was strictly for their luggage! Trust me...10 women who are packing for a 4 day trip can pack more than 20 men going on a one month trip!!

Mary Kay still has their yearly events and I still miss seeing those ladies! They may be running Mary Kay for all I know now!! I kind of hope they are!!

Mohamed Ali-The Champ

I got a call one day about lunch time from some restaurant clients of mine directing me to go over to a certain hotel and pick up someone for them over there. They didn't tell me who it was, just that they would be waiting out front, and that I would recognize them! That's pretty intriguing for anyone!

When I got to the hotel, I saw an entourage of people gathered outside....and he was right, I did recognize...one of my heroes, Mohamed Ali!! I had been in the business long enough that I wasn't as star-struck as I had been years earlier, but Mohamed Ali got me a little star-struck!

I took him and his entourage to the restaurant for a very interesting lunch! Mohamed Ali was sitting in the middle of the table among all of his friends and people gathered there. He spoke very softly so you really had to listen closely to hear what he was saying. You could tell a little bit that his health was slightly beginning to decline, but he was still just as funny and entertaining as ever. After a while, he raised his fist in the air and took a silk handkerchief and said he was going to make it disappear! He began stuffing the handkerchief in his fist...and then he opened his hand...and it had disappeared!! Everyone was amazed! He said he was going to do it again! So, he did it again! After the second time, everyone had to know how he made it disappear. He started laughing uncontrollably and pulled off a fake thumb!! He was stuffing the handkerchief in the fake thumb!

One of the traditions of the restaurant was that each celebrity guest would sign a bottle of champagne that they kept in their trophy case. When they brought him a bottle of champagne to sign, he said he couldn't sign a bottle of alcohol (against his religious beliefs), so in a little while, they brought in a box of Cuban cigars and he signed the box. The entire trophy case is full of bottles of champagne…and one box of cigars!

This event with Mohamed Ali took place during the O.J. Simpson trial. You can imagine there was a lot of interesting conversations going on about the trial. To my surprise, everyone was using the "N" word! Finally, he spoke up and said, "If you have never used the 'N' word, I want you to raise your hand!" Not a single person in the group raised their hand! He said, "That's what I thought, whether you're black or white, you've used that word!"

I got to have my picture taken with him and he autographed it, "I had fun, George!" After he got through eating, I took him back to his hotel, but that is one of my favorite days because I was so proud I got to drive Mohamed Ali! He was really a great guy!

Name Dropper-
Just to Name a Few

I have mentioned many times through out this book how very thankful and blessed I was to be able to work with all 26 radio stations in the DFW area! That allowed me to meet celebrities from all different genres and all different walks of life!

I'm not going to write a story about all of these people; I'm just going to drop a few names of some of the long list of incredible people I got to meet and even became friends with some of them!

- ⊗ Guns & Roses
- ⊗ Pantera
- ⊗ Red Hot Chili Peppers
- ⊗ Cher
- ⊗ AC/DC
- ⊗ Fu Fighters
- ⊗ Tony Bennett
- ⊗ Kelly Clarkson
- ⊗ Steven Tyler
- ⊗ KISS

And this list doesn't even scratch the surface of all of the great people I got to meet!

The most amazing thing about all of this is that I actually got *paid* to meet these people!

How lucky can one person be? I don't consider it luck! I consider it a blessing!

New Year's Eve 1999!

*I*f you *remember* New Year's Eve 1999, then I'm sure you remember all of the scary rumors that were going around about Y2K! Some people thought the world was coming to an end and all sorts of horrible things were going to happen! However, most normal people didn't have a clue *why* people were anticipating such crazy things were going to happen!

So, I had 10 people scheduled to be picked up about 10 o'clock on that New Year's Eve. I was totally surprised when they all showed up with extremely packed duffle bags! Yes, I said…duffle bags! You know those long cylindrical bags that are about four feet long and typically are used by the military when they are being deployed for a long time! All 10 people had a duffle bag that we had to stuff in the limo, along with 10 people! The trunk was full and the entire area next to me up front was completely packed with…duffle bags! I wondered what in the world did they have planned to do with them…and did I mention they were all packed full!

Needless to say, I was curious to see where they were going to want to go. To my surprise, they wanted to go to a spot about 30 miles outside of town…right in the middle of nowhere! Strangely enough, they got out of the limo and just walked around and talked among themselves, but there was certainly **NO** celebrating going on! It seems this group of somewhat misguided people had bought into the hype that the world was ending, buildings were going to explode, computers were going to stop working…and nothing was going to be like…before!

Even though the world *didn't* end, most of those people actually seemed a little disappointed that things were going to go on as usual! Personally, I was ecstatic that everything was staying the same!

After the non-climactic midnight, we drove the 30 miles back into Dallas, and as expected, the city was full of the usual lights and excitement of New Year's Eve! The streets were full of happy people celebrating the New Year! The New Year of 2000! We were beginning a new century! How exciting was that?

I have often wondered how those 10 people have coped with living in the new century since they were so sure it would not happen! I hope they see all of the wonderful things that have been created since the year 2000! I hope that they have learned to look outside of themselves and their fears to see the beautiful world that is around them! And if they are still living in the most wonderful country on Earth, America, I hope they realize how truly blessed they are!

Oh, What a Night...!
多麼夜啊.....!

The average person would not believe all of the different types of people there are in the world and who come to visit and play in Dallas! It still boggles my mind and _**I was there!**_

Dallas is noted for all of the different types of commerce that is drawn to the city because of its patchwork of cultures that had settled there from all over the world! One of my funniest and most interesting set of clients was a group of Chinese businessmen who were in Dallas for a major business meeting with the American portion of their company.

One of the most enjoyable perks of working with the Cabaret Royale was that I got to meet and mingle with most of the employees of the club, many of whom were the dancers! On this particular night, I was sitting in the parking lot of the club waiting for the time to take my Chinese businessmen back to their hotel after their night of fun and "frolicking!" Since I was waiting in my limo behind the club, I saw one of the young dancers come out the back door and she looked like she was crying! Being the gentleman I was, I got out and called to her. As she got closer, my instinct was correct as she was crying! I'll just call her Dawn.

I inquired as to why Dawn was crying and she told me that she had not made enough money that night to pay her rent! And to make it worse, if she was late with her rent, she would have to pay an extra $50 per day! (That would be enough to make me cry too....and extra $50 per day!) I could tell she needed to talk to someone, so I told her to get up in the front of the limo with me so she could talk...and we did. In about half an hour, I received the notice that my clients were out front and ready to be picked up. As I cranked up the car and headed to the front of the club, I asked her if she wanted to ride with me while I took them back to their hotel and I would bring her back to the club. By this time, she had stopped crying and agreed to ride with me.

All eight of the Chinese businessmen were "excited" when they got back in the limo. They were all smiling from ear to ear and chattering in Chinese… .你看到那些大咪咪了嗎！That was Chinese for…. "Did you see all of those BIG boobs?"

When I got back in the driver's seat in the front of the limo where Dawn was, I had an idea. Since the men were all so "happy," I asked Dawn if she wanted to crawl through the window between the driver's seat and the limo to see if she might be able to make some money. Her eyes lit up and she said… "I believe I do!"….and she did! Once she was in the back of the limo, I closed the window, but I could still hear even louder laughter coming from the back!

In a few minutes, Dawn, with a big grin on her grin on her face told me to drive slowly back to the hotel….which I did! Finally, after about 45 minutes of "driving slow", she came back to the window and told me I could go on to their hotel now!

When we pulled up to the front of their hotel, I got out of the front to let them exit the limo. I just thought they had big smiles when they came out of the club, but they weren't half as animated as their smiles were now!! They were all so exuberant that each one of them gave me a large tip on top of their regular fare! By this time, Dawn had exited the back of the limo and gotten back up front.

By this time…she was definitely NOT crying, but had a smile as big as the Chinese men had had on their faces. It seems she had made an extra $1600 on the ride to the hotel from the businessmen. Her account of the *"limo events"* was that she had offered each of them an *individual "service"* and they agreed with great anticipation! However, none of them could "perform" but pretended that they were enjoying it to the fullest…to save face with their co-horts! ***So Dawn made an extra $200 from each man by basically….doing nothing!!***

I'm sure that these same Chinese businessmen were my repeat customers the next time they came back to Dallas! However, they never had another adventure like they did their first night in Dallas with *Limo George*!

"Oil for One" and "One for Oil" (Sorry, No Speak Engless!)

I would imagine any time you are in another country and you don't speak the language of that country, you're not going to have as much fun as you would if you could communicate while you are there!

Difficulty communicating with a Hispanic band was just the beginning of the problems I had with a bus trip to Waco with this international group of musicians!

I had just purchased a used bus to add to my fleet of transportation vehicles when I was contacted about taking a band of Mexican musicians for their performance that was coming up in Waco, Texas. The money was definitely going to be good although I did not speak any Spanish...I figured I could probably fake it pretty well! After all, working in the public in Dallas all my life, I had picked up a few expressions that I could understand. (Some I probably wish I didn't know, but at times even those came in handy!) So... I accepted the assignment!

Again, just to reiterate what I stated before...I had just purchased a used bus to expand my transportation capabilities! Because I had this bus, it gave me more confidence in agreeing to transport this band to Waco! (Looking back, that was absolutely a false assumption on my part!)

The band arrived at DFW airport late one evening with their instruments and luggage where I picked them up and took them to their hotel. I was to pick them up there the next morning for the 1 hour and 45 minute trip to Waco, Texas.

The trip down was relatively uneventful. Actually it was rather pleasant! There was a lot of laughing and talking and even a brief concert for me as they practiced some of their songs for their show! I believe the songs performed acoustically were my favorite!

When we arrived in Waco, I took the group to their hotel for them to rest, eat, and to get ready for their performance later that evening. I personally love Waco, so I enjoyed just visiting some of my favorite stores, shops, and restaurants until I had to pick them up.

Their performance was excellent! I must say that practice they had on my bus really did prepare them for their performance! (I'm kidding about that!)

After the concert, I took them out to dinner and then to their hotel for the night. The one man who spoke English told me I would need to pick them up at about 9:00 A.M. to make sure they were back at the DFW airport in time for their 1:00 P.M. flight! Since it was only about a 1 hour and 45 minute trip that a 9:00 pick up would give us *plenty* of time to make their flight! ***Little…*** ***.did….I….know!!***

The next morning, I brought the bus around about 8:30 in case anyone was ready early they could load their luggage and instruments and be ready to leave at 9:00 sharp! But as the old saying goes – ***the Best Laid Plans of Mice and Men oft go awry…and that is exactly what happened!!*** While waiting for the men to arrive and load I noticed that my check oil light came on. That is never a good sign! I got a sick feeling in the pit of my stomach when I saw that…but I hoped a quart of oil would take care of the problem! ***Wrong!***

After everyone was on the bus and we started back to Dallas, I decided, I needed to stop and get a few quarts of oil to put in the bus…just in case. **Well, that** *'just in case'* **turned out to be about** *2 cases of oil!!* For every 20 miles we drove, the bus burned about 4 quarts of oil! It's a wonder we weren't stopped by the highway patrol as a road hazard simply because of all the smoke the bus was putting out!

What made the situation even worse was that you couldn't put the oil in from under the hood on the top of the motor, you had to crawl under the bus to add the oil!! WE STOPPED AT LEAST 4 TIMES TO ADD OIL!

I have to give credit where credit is due. The Hispanic guys were buying oil *and* getting under the bus to help me put the oil in! I never figured out if they were just that helpful, or if they were just that afraid they would miss their flight and be stuck on the side of the road with me!!

The last straw came as we were coming across the last bridge on DFW Airport just before we turned into the terminal loading area....and it stopped....dead....for the last time!!! By this time, it was almost time for them to actually be boarding their flight! These poor guys, even though they were exhausted from the trip back from Waco they had to grab their luggage and instruments and started walking/running down to the terminal!!!

Before I got off that bus, I called the low-down weasel I had bought it from and told him to come and get it and give me my money back! I, too, left that bus on the bridge at DFW airport....and I never saw it...or the Mexican band again!!

While I would like to have seen the band perform again, I'm sure they would have all run in the other direction if they saw me coming...and I can't blame them!!

Pat Summerall

I had the honor of picking up Pat Summerall at his home in Dallas and taking him to an event where he was being honored by the radio station KRLD/CBS. At that time, he had a big beautiful home in Dallas where he had settled with his wife after his NFL career ended and his career began in sports casting.

The event took place in the Dallas Arboretum which is located near downtown Dallas and backs up to White Rock Lake (which is a man-made lake). The event to honor Pat was hosted by the Dallas Radio Station KRLD shortly after his retirement from sports casting.

It was a star-studded event with lots of NFL players in attendance. I got to talk to Dallas Cowboys greats such as Roger Staubach and Troy Aikman which is always interesting for a Dallas Cowboys fan, which I definitely am!

As the evening ended, and I returned Pat home, his wife was waiting at the front door. It reminded me that even when people are in the public eye, *home* is always the BEST place to be...no matter what!

Police – 4th of July – Parade – Prosper

*W*hat do those four things have in common? Well, if you lived… .in Prosper, Texas, which was a small town at one time, you probably would get to know the police officers there. As you would imagine, since it was a small town, the police force was small as well so by default, you might get to know *all* of the officers there (all 10 of them) …which could be a good thing…or maybe a bad thing…of course that would depend entirely on *you!*

Then that brings us to the parade, on the 4th of July…which was really a big deal in a small town. It was not easy to even get out to Prosper at that time. It was a long way from anywhere! But once you got there, it was a little slice of heaven! Little things were a big deal in a small town like Prosper. One really big and notable event was when they actually added the first red light! That was significant because there were only about 6 or 7 blocks in the whole downtown area of Prosper!

Even little things are big in small towns. And, for the most part, everyone in town that was able, would participate in the events (whatever they would be) so a parade was one of those ***little "big things!"***

On this particular 4th of July, I, Limo George, got to lead the parade in one of my limos! The parade stretched for about 5 blocks considering there were about 1 and ½ car lengths between each vehicle! The crowd lined both sides of the street, shouting and waving flags! We even got to go through the signal light when it was red! The parade would drive down to the junior high school at one end of town and then turn around and slowly drive back through town to the elementary school at the other end of town.

It sounds corny now, but back then, it was what good, clean fun was made of! You didn't have to worry about school shootings or being ambushed at a movie theater, or being shot at a concert. Those simple times in small towns like Prosper, for all of the people who were lucky enough to get to live there then, will always be cherished memories. I know that simple way of life might have seemed a little dull at times back then, but looking back, those were some of the best...and simplest times of my life!

Just a note: I got to know some of the Prosper police officers when I discovered I had a snake on my back porch. I called the police for help. The next thing I know, three police cars pulled up at my house with their lights on. When the snake was apprehended, they had it in a pillow case and it was less than 3 feet long...and harmless! It took me a while to live that one down, but it was the start of a great friendship with the Prosper Police Department and it may have even led to me getting to lead the 4th of July parade!

Radio Games with Chris Jagger
102.1 The Edge

*A*s I have mentioned before, I had the unique opportunity to work with all 26 radio stations in the Dallas/Ft. Worth area and I had some really fun and interesting adventures with some of them.

One of my favorite on-air personalities was Chris Jagger on 102.1 The Edge. As the name of the station indicated, their programming was a little edgy, which turned into some enjoyable times for me!

I actually got to participate on-air with two different games with Disc Jockey Chris Jagger on Friday mornings! Part of his Friday morning show included The Dating Game and The Price Is Right. Of course, the games were set up specifically for their show and they weren't quite the same as the original television shows!

For The Dating Game, contestants would call the station on Thursday afternoon to sign up to hopefully get chosen to play the game the next morning. The concept was similar to the original in that the female that was chosen would think of three questions she would like to ask the three males that she would get to choose from for her weekend date. The program director would *listen* to the female callers to select the one that would be Friday's contestant. Once he selected her, he would give me a call and give me the address to pick her up the next morning and take her to the studio for the game for the show at 7:00 A.M.

When we started walking into the studio where Chris was, the fun began! The three guys were on hold on the telephone lines so they couldn't hear anything that was being said. The woman would be walking in behind me so she couldn't see or hear anything either. Chris would say, "Well, Limo George is here with our contestant for this morning and he is giving us thumbs up (or thumbs down)!" Of course, that meant whether she was good looking...or not so good looking! (We eventually found out that the program director wasn't interviewing the contestants to pick the best one, he was picking them by the one with the sexiest voice! That didn't always mean she was pretty!!)

Once the contestant was seated and given her headset, the game would begin. She would ask each of the three guys her three questions. The one that she liked their answers best would be the one she would get a date with for that night!

After The Dating Game was over the next game was The Price Is Right! The twist to this one was that they would take a common item and they would write a description of the item using as many long, complicated, hard to pronounce words as they could find. The kicker was that I had to read the description of the item and callers would try and guess what the item was and how much it would cost. The hilarious part of the game was my efforts to read the concocted description they had written! I always read it on the air for the first time. I was always surprised when anyone was able to guess what the item was! I'm certain they had to take a long time looking through the dictionary to find some of the words they put in those descriptions! Of course, I was the brunt of much laughter and teasing.

When we finished with the games, I would take the female contestant back home and then get started with the rest of my day. We had this schedule for a couple of years, every Friday. I never got tired of the time I spent working with Chris Jagger. He was one of the nicest guys you would ever want to meet.

Russ Martin-DJ at The Eagle

I was fortunate enough or blessed enough to work with **ALL 26 radio stations** in the Dallas-Ft. Worth area almost from the beginning of my limo business. The fact that I worked with all of the stations was a miracle within itself because none of them could get along with each other because they were all in competition with each other! I enjoyed getting to be part of the transportation for the stations and all of the celebrities that came into town to the stations, but at times I also got to play bodyguard for some of them!! (What can I say…I've just got a winning personality…and great smile!)

When you are working with people, it's hard not to make friends with them. That's what happened with a DJ named Russ Martin. He had a Sunday night talk show on The Eagle Radio Station. I was working one Sunday night and I was tuned into The Eagle and heard Russ talking about the terrible food at the Gentlemen's clubs in Dallas. Fortunately, that was a subject I knew a lot about…not because *I* frequented them, but I did take a *lot* of businessmen who were visiting Dallas to them!

After listening to him put down the food at the clubs, I concluded he obviously had never visited one! I called into the show that night to dispute what he was saying. I think he was amazed that anyone would so vehemently defend the food at the gentlemen's clubs like I did. I gave him my number and we arranged for me to pick him and his date up the next week to go try out the food at the clubs!

As planned, I picked Russ and his date up and took them to the Cabaret Royale for supper. Not only did they get to enjoy an amazing meal, but a friendship was started that lasted many years that included many fun and interesting events.

After that night, Russ could tell his audience that the food at the gentlemen's clubs could rival those of most 5-star restaurants! Looking back now, the clubs probably got a good boost in business because of the free advertisement they got from Russ after that night! Sometimes it's a win-win for everybody!

Russ Martin Story #2 – Batman Returns

*M*ost people that knew Russ knew that he was a huge Batman enthusiast! He had tons of Batman memorabilia which even included a Batman cape, mask....and yes....even *a replica of the Batmobile!!* All of his listeners knew that was kind of his signature thing!

Eventually, Russ was dismissed from the The Eagle and went to work at The Fan radio station for a couple of years. When The Eagle decided to bring Russ back, he decided to do something to let his listeners know he was coming back. This was one of the fun things I got to do with him....we took a large spotlight and were able to beam the Batman emblem on the side of The Eagle radio station building the night before Russ was to start broadcasting again! His fans all loved it and knew that *Russ was back!!!*

Russ Martin Story #3 – Running Naked

*A*s most Disc Jockeys do, Russ was always having local and famous celebrities and sports figures on his show on a regular basis. I was one of his regular local celebrities! Russ and I would do "Limo Talk" where I would tell him things that happened in the limo business over the last week. Some things were funny and interesting and sometimes, there wasn't much to report. On one Sunday evening, he had one of the Dallas Stars hockey players on his show. Russ always was thinking of ways to challenge his guests so he told the hockey player that *if he knocked an opponent down in the next game and stood over him and flapped his arms like an eagle, that he would do whatever the hockey player wanted him to do!* The player agreed and he decided that he would want Russ to run across the Tollway...*naked!!* As luck would have it, the hockey player knocked an opponent down, flapped has arms like an eagle...and *now*...Russ and his then sidekick, Valerie, had to run across the Tollway...*naked!!*

On the day Russ had to carry out his part of the challenge, there were hundreds of people lining the fence alongside the Tollway at the radio station. There were people everywhere waiting to see Russ...and his female sidekick cross the Tollway...naked! The police were there for crowd control and to protect the runners! I had devised a plan where three limos would drive side by side down the tollway blocking all three lanes. They would stop in front of the radio station. Russ would jump out of one limo (naked) and run to the next limo beside it and get in. His sidekick would jump out of another limo (naked) and get into the one beside her. And then they would swap again. As soon as the swapping was completed, all three limos took off and when they got to I-635, they all went in different directions in case anyone was trying to follow them, they wouldn't know which limo they were in. **MISSION ACCOM-PLISHED!!! CHALLENGE MET!!!** That was a really FUN DAY!!

Russ Martin Story #4 – Russ and The Band

*A*s our friendship grew, I learned that Russ was one of the truly genuine great human beings! He used to offer his celebrity status as often and as much as possible to help anyone that needed help. Some of the people closest to his heart were the fallen and injured policemen, firemen, and EMTs; any of the first responders who were hurt or killed in the line of duty! Russ put on events to raise money for them and their families before it was "cool" to do so!

He started his own band and it was billed as the Russ Martin Show. Before each show, I would pick him up in a limo and take him to the venue where he was to play. Almost always, there would be police officers waiting to escort him (us) into the green room for him to get ready for the show. I was the only individual that he would allow in there with him until he went on stage. I never took that privilege for granted….and I did consider it a privilege!

Russ raised a tremendous amount of money for the families of the first responders. On the day any one of them was killed in the line of duty, he would write them a check for at least $30,000 so they would have money immediately to live on until their other sources of income became available!

To this day, Russ is still working and serving in the Dallas/Ft. Worth area at The Eagle! Tune in and listen to him sometime. Tell him Limo George said hello!

Russ Martin
and the Austin Bats

*R*uss Martin was and is one of the legends in the radio business in Dallas for decades. Most of his listeners very easily associate bats with Russ Martin since he is a died-in-the-wool Batman fan even down to having a replica of the BATMOBILE!! So, it was very fitting that his radio station had a contest to be able to go in a limo down to Austin, Texas, to see the bats fly!

I had no clue what in the world going to watch the **bats fly in Austin** involved, but I personally didn't care since I was given the job...and I was going to ***Austin to watch the bats fly!***

As with most radio contests, there was more than a little liquor consumed on the trip from Dallas to Austin! I can truthfully say that in talking with most of the winners of the contest, they had no idea what they were going to witness in Austin. They were just planning on partying there and back. And, if they saw something interesting, that was just a perk of the trip!

The trip was planned so that we got to Austin a couple of hours before sunset, so we had a little time to kill before the big event! We all were very skeptical that watching bats fly was really going to be a big event, but it was basically a *free trip* and a *party!*

I was completely surprised that parking near the ***Congress Avenue Bridge*** (the purported sight of the flight) was pretty crowded! If my memory serves me correctly, this momentous event took place in late August, so you can imagine, it was *hot* in Austin, Texas!

As the sun started to set and the sky began turning tones of red, orange, yellow, and pink, we began to hear a low rustle of what we soon began to realize was bat wings! The rustling got louder, and louder, and louder! The louder the noise got, the blacker the sky got as the bats began their nightly hunt! The bats kept taking flight from under the bridge! ***It was one of the most amazing sights I have ever seen!!***

The sight was breathtaking!! BATS!! Who knew nature could create such a spectacular sight from under a bridge!! Even though quite a bit of liquid courage had been consumed between Dallas and Austin, that sight was pretty sobering!! Needless to say there was a lot of discussion on the trip home about what we had seen!

Here are just a few facts about the bats in Austin! They come up from Mexico in March of each year. By the end of August, the colony of Mexican Free-Tail Bats typically grows to an estimated 1.5 million. The city of Austin welcomes their nocturnal visitors because of the service they do for property owners by devouring unwanted insects in the Austin area.

Russ Martin- Drag Racing

I had a lot of opportunities to do things with Russ Martin, one of the legendary DJs in the Dallas area at 97.1, The Eagle.

One adventure I got to go on with Russ was one day when he was going to be a drag racer as a promotion for the radio station.

It was extremely fun to get to park in the area with all the dragsters and drivers and get to meet ones that I had watched and heard of for years!

I was completely amazed at how it seemed like the crews for the dragsters could disassemble them, clean them up and re-assemble them in about 30 minutes! That was mind blowing considering how complex and complicated those dragsters are! I believe the thing that got my attention was how very *loud* those vehicles are! The drivers and the crew members all had to wear ear protection to protect their hearing from the excessive noise levels associated with the dragsters!

I'm pretty sure that Russ did not win his drag race, but I'm sure he had fun with the experience! I know I surely did!

Russ Martin-LaBare

*M*y dear friend, Russ Martin, who is a DJ at The Eagle radio station in Dallas, is always looking for ways to raise money to support the first responders in the Dallas/Ft. Worth area. One of his ideas was to meet with Master Blaster from La Bare to see what it would take for him to become a guest dancer at the club to raise money for his favorite group, first responders! They both loved the idea, so the planning began.

Russ lived in Frisco, so every Saturday for a month, he had me to pick him up at home and take him to a gym in Southlake to work out. He wanted to *get into shape* so he would look more like the dancers! I kept telling him that round is a shape but he wasn't into just being round!

The night finally came, and he was a nervous wreck! He was afraid of several things:

1. No one would show up to see him,
2. A lot of people would show up to see him,
3. He wouldn't raise any/much money,
4. He would look stupid (after all, he had a reputation to maintain!).

When we pulled up to the club, the parking lot was absolutely packed! There had been a tremendous amount of publicity for the night and it had paid off. To Russ that was a really good thing and a scary, bad thing! Even though hesitant, Cowboy Russ got out and headed into his La Bare history night!

At 10:00, it was time for Russ to go on! The music began, the lights came up, and Russ began the dance! The room was packed with screaming women who were ready for Cowboy Russ! Of course, the more he danced the more clothes he took off and the louder the room got. Money began raining down on Cowboy Russ! I could see that the more he danced the more fun he was having and the looser he got! By the time the music ended, Russ was having a blast!! He raised an enormous amount of money for his favorite people, the Dallas/Ft. Worth first responders!

After all the money was picked up and counted, we were ready for me to take Russ home. We had a certain ritual that we always followed on the way home from an event. Russ always had me to stop by a Jack in the Box fast food place to get 14 tacos. That was 12 tacos for Russ and 2 tacos for me!

I failed to mention that in order to get his courage up before he had to dance, Russ managed to have a few drinks along the way! So, with his liquid courage and the relief of completing his La Bare dance, Russ was feeling no pain! As a matter of fact, when we got to his gated subdivision, he couldn't re-member the code to the gate to get in! This was really a problem since that time of the morning, there were no other cars going in or out that we could follow in when the gate was opened!

There were 2 entrances, one off of the toll road and one off of Legacy Drive. He even tried to climb over the fence, but he was unable to. We thought we had lucked out at the Legacy entrance and we were sitting there hoping a car would come up that we could follow in. A car did come up and stopped. However, it was not a friendly person that stopped. Come to find out it was the HOA manager and he was very angry that we were trying to get in the gate without the code or a card. Russ (being slightly inebriated), tried to ex-plain he lived there and forgot the code, but the guy said he did not recognize him! I thought they were going to come to blows!! I finally told them they needed to stop because I had called the police!

Mr. HOA manager got in his car and sped off. Russ got back in the limo and we tried to follow him to the other entrance to follow him in, but he beat us and the gate closed. In a last ditch effort, Russ shoved his box of tacos under the gate. Then he managed to climb OVER the gate, picked up his box of tacos and started walking to his house…about ½ mile away. I'll never forget how much he looked like a little boy…walking down the middle of the street among the million dollar homes in his shorts, T-shirt, and flip flops, eating tacos! If anyone happened to look out their window, they would not have even guessed that a La Bare dancer was walking down their street!!

Russ Martin
Police-Fire Fighter-
First Responder Parade

*A*merica is THE greatest nation on Earth, and one of the things that makes it SO great is the fact that we have the greatest police officers, fire fighters, and first responders in the entire world!! Their bravery is unequaled!

One of my favorite people in the Dallas area is DJ Russ Martin at The Eagle. I have mentioned him a few times regarding all of the benevolent things Russ has done for the Dallas area and the parade honoring the first responders was just another one of the ways he was able to show respect and support for them.

This parade became a yearly event and was supported by all of the area police precincts, fire departments, and ambulance companies. A date was selected and all of the groups were notified. The parade would begin in the parking lot of the American Airlines Center. If you have never been there, it is huge! I would be the lead car in the parade with Russ in the limo. The parade would be miles and miles long with car after car of police vehicles, fire trucks, and engine company cars and ambulances, all with lights flashing! What a sight that was!!

The best part about the parade was that the residents of Dallas were all along the parade route cheering on the participants as they drove by. The love and respect for all of the police officers, fire fighters, and first responders was absolutely amazing! It almost gives me chill bumps now thinking about what an amazing sight it was to see the miles of red, white, and blue lights flashing as the parade slowly snaked along the parade route!

The first year the parade left the American Airlines Center and made its way to Texas Stadium where all of the participating vehicles wound up parking so that a picture could be taken of all of them. However, there were so many vehicles in the parade that by the time we reached Texas Stadium, there were still vehicles that had not been able to leave the American Airlines Center parking lot! The second year, the parade was extended from the AA Center to the Lone Star Park, which is the horse racing track in Grand Prairie! This extended parade route not only allowed all of the cars to be able to get out of the parking lot, but to make it to the finish and to be able to participate in the festivities that many of the police stations provided at the end! Most of the time it looked and felt like a really large tail-gate party that the police precincts put on to show appreciation to Russ for all that he did to honor and support them!

As I mentioned in a previous story, because of his fund-raising efforts, at one time, Russ Martin was able to write a check for $35,000 on the spot when there was a fallen police officer in the Dallas/Ft. Worth area! Russ and I love the police and have had an ongoing passion for all first responders because of the selfless work they do for their communities every time they put on their uniform and punch the clock.

If you can lay down and go to sleep and not worry whether your family is safe, thank a police officer. If you know that if you had a fire or natural disaster and there would be someone to call, thank a fire fighter. If you had an accident or a medical emergency at home and know that there is someone that is within minutes to take care of you, thank a first responder! If you live in America, you are blessed beyond measure! If you are thankful for your freedom, thank a soldier!!

Santa George-
Arcadia Elementary

*W*e see in the world today mostly through the eyes of the media the hatred and mistrust among people of all nationalities and races and groups! But we all know that there are still so many good people in the world and so much good in the world and even just next door, and that is what makes life worth living every day!

One of the fun and rewarding things I was blessed to be able to do was to play Santa at the Arcadia Elementary School in Oak Cliff, which was an under privileged area of Dallas. A few weeks before Christmas, in conjunction with the principal, teachers, and school board for the school, I would start collecting toys. They would describe how many children were enrolled and about some of the needs of some of the families.

By the time the week of Christmas would roll around, Santa George, and his elves would have collected and wrapped enough toys and gifts so that each child would have at least one gift! I would have two or three limos full of toys and gifts! I would arrange a time with the school for us to come deliver the toys. Everyone would be assembled in the auditorium.

My elves and I would bring all of the wrapped gifts in and stack them all around Santa George's chair that was already in place! The excitement was so thick in the air you could just about cut it with a knife! The joy on all of those little faces was almost overwhelming to us!

The principal would quiet everyone down and then line them up from the youngest to the oldest! As the line started by Santa George, I would hand each one of them a wrapped present! The sparkle in their eyes and the grins on

149

their faces was priceless! The thing was, it didn't matter what the present was, and the children were thrilled that someone (Santa George) was giving them something! For some of those children, that may have been the only gift they got for Christmas!

One year I partnered with Speed Zone and they filled one of the drag cars with presents and brought it for the children to see as well! That day was a really big hit too!

Being Santa George at Arcadia Elementary School will always be one of my fondest Christmas memories because of being able to put smiles on all of those beautiful little faces at a time some of them might not have had much to smile about!

Wrapped presents and gifts at Christmas are fun and nice, but in the world we live in today, even the gift of your smile, a kind word, a hug, or a gentle touch may have an eternal effect on someone that you may never even realize that you made! Be generous with your kindness!

Seeing Stars-
Dallas Stars, That Is!

*T*hrough the years I have provided transportation for many of the Dallas Stars for various events as well as for their personal needs. I have found an interesting fact about most famous people is that when it comes down to it…they are just like regular people! Whether athletes, movie or media stars, or whatever their celebrity may be, they all sooner or later just want to let their hair down and be just regular people.

Craig Ludwig was a Dallas Stars Hockey player that loved to go 4 wheeling. The best I could tell he would sneak out of the house after his wife went to sleep to enjoy his hobby and then around 2 o'clock in the morning, he would call me to come pick him up and take him home. I would stop about a half block from his house. He would take his shoes off and tip toe back into the house to keep from waking his wife up! As far as I know, it must have worked! I never heard of him receiving any injuries from his wife from sneaking in at 2 A.M. in the morning! After all of these years, I wonder if he ever outgrew his need for speed or if he is still sneaking out to play!

Another Dallas Stars player I used to pick up a lot was Derian Hatcher. Hatcher led the Stars to their first Stanley Cup in franchise history in 1999 to become the first American-born captain of a Stanley Cup winning team. After winning the Stanley Cup, each team member got to keep the trophy for a certain number of days and do whatever they wanted to with it. One thing Derian wanted to do with it was to drive it around Dallas in a limo… that was my limo! It was very exciting to get to actually see the Stanley Cup up close and touch it!

My daughter, Ana, was a huge Derian Hatcher fan! One day he had called me to drive him to the airport. I was unable to because of previous commitments so I called Ana to drive him for me. As fathers do, I asked her if she could please help me out that day by taking someone to the airport for me. Her immediate answer was an emphatic, "NO! I'm not doing that anymore!" I, of course, said, "Please again one more time"...and still got another "NO!" Then, I said, "I guess I'll just have to tell Derian Hatcher we can't do it!" IMMEDIATELY her schedule changed and she could take HIM to the airport! (Kids!) After she picked him up, she called me and was whispering, "Dad, he's in the car...and I can see him in the mirror!" She was so excited! He even autographed a hockey puck for her which I imagine she still has to this very day! I can laugh now because I finally found a way to push her buttons and change her NO to a BIG OL' YES!!

Ed Belfour was another Dallas Stars player I enjoyed driving for! As part of the Stanley Cup Stars Team, Ed also got to keep the Stanley Cup for his allotted time. He too wanted to drive with it around Dallas in a limo...my limo, but Ed had had a little bit too much to drink during and before the ride. His idea of fun was to stand up in the open moon roof and hold the Stanley Cup over his head while we were moving! I personally thought that might be a little risky for that prized cup, so I slowed down and stopped. Not to have his fun spoiled, Ed climbed out of the moon roof with trophy in hand and proceeded to walk down the length of the limo from the opening down the top, down the windshield, then down the hood! Needless to say, it was not cheap having all of the dents removed from the top and hood of the limo, but Ed didn't seem to mind since he was having fun showing off the Stanley Cup while it was "his!"

Short and Sweet (Sex)

*T*here are some things in life that you just can't explain or understand regardless of how hard you try! Some things just make you scratch your head and go....huh?

I was sitting at home one Sunday afternoon when I got a call from a man asking if I would rent my limo for an hour. I told him I was sorry, but my minimum was four hours and I gave him the price. He thanked me and hung up. A few minutes later, he called back and said he would pay the full four hour price, but he still just needed an hour.

I told him I would be happy to pick him up; just tell me where and when. To my surprise, he wanted me to pick him and his wife up at their hotel... within the hour. I told him I wasn't dressed, (I was at home watching the Cowboys playing football) but I would be out shortly!

I picked the two of them up within the hour at their hotel. When they met me in the lobby, he paid me for the full four hours as we had agreed. As I looked around at his wife, I realized that she was carrying a pillow and blanket!

As I helped them into the back of the limo, I asked him where they wanted to go. He winked at me and told me that it really didn't matter...that it had always been his wife's fantasy to have sex in a limo...and this was her anniversary present! He still assured me that they would only need it for an hour! (I couldn't help but smile to myself!)

Since we were in downtown Dallas, I decided I would drive out to the Dallas/Ft. Worth Airport, turn around and then drive back. That should take about an hour!

The only problem with that scenario was that about 20 minutes into the drive, I got a call from the back of the limo…they were ready to go back to the hotel!! I knew at that point, some fantasies don't take very long to be fulfilled!!

Stars Staff Comes Out to Party

*Y*ou have heard about Quid Pro Quo…well, I got to do a lot of that in my line of work! I was fortunate enough to have been given concert and sporting event tickets from different companies and I was able to use those perks to share with the other people who so often shared with me! Life is better when it is shared!!

One time I had been given a lot of tickets to a Rangers game and I decided I would take the sales staff from the Stars and treat them to the game! I'm not sure if they were excited about getting to actually go to a Rangers game or whether it was just the thought of getting to go to the game on a party bus….and *party!*

On the day of the game, it was really hot!! ***I'm talking about really Texas hot!!*** But, no one seemed to actually care about the heat! They decided they were going to have a tailgate party besides the party bus…complete with a grill, food, and all the trimmings! Man was that fun! The great part of about that tailgate party was that I got to participate too! The food was great, and everybody was having fun, fun, fun! It was strange seeing these particular people dancing, drinking, and singing because I was used to seeing them in their usual business attire of suits and ties and dress up clothes! ***But party they did!!***

When it was time for the game, I doubt if many people could even remember if the Rangers won or lost! I know I couldn't remember!

Let's just say the Rangers won!! Once we got back to the bus and got everything loaded and ready to go, I discovered that of all things, the bus wouldn't start! The battery was dead! Some nice people who were parked next to us were kind enough to jump the battery off…and we were on our way back to Frisco….in the heat! Unfortunately, because of the heat, I was concerned the strain of the air conditioner on the battery might cause it to go dead again, so we made the trip…without any cool air! I've got to hand it to the Stars sales staff, they were real troopers!

They continued to have fun all the way back to Frisco even in the sweltering heat! They said they were there to party.. and that's exactly what they did…even in the hot, Texas heat!

State Fair of Texas-Free Pass Radio Station

*A*s I have mentioned before, there were 26 radio stations in the Dallas/Ft. Worth area, and I had the unusual privilege of working with all of them. Along with working with all of them, one of the perks I got was a pass to get into the State Fair of Texas. It was basically for my car, but whoever was in the car or vehicle with me could get into the fair free! As you can imagine, that was a pretty sweet deal!

I was out there most weekend during the fair, especially for the Texas/OU game which was a big deal for the Dallas area. We would usually have some sort of a tailgate party out there whether the group I was taking out there was in a limo or a party bus. There was always a party going on during the big game weekend at the fair.

One weekend I wasn't going to use the radio pass so I let one of my drivers use it. I feel certain that I had told him exactly how the pass worked as far as a car or maybe a party bus. However, later on during the weekend, I got a call from one of my main contacts at this particular radio station and he was furious!! It seems that my driver had a full Greyhound size bus full of people, who, by the way DID NOT SPEAK ENGLISH, and had taken them into the fair!

Oh…the fair officials were livid!! They told me I had 30 minutes to round ALL of those people up, get them on the BUS, and get them off of the fairgrounds! What made it even worse was I WASN'T ANYWHERE NEAR THE FAIRGROUNDS! I don't even like to think about all it took to try and gather all those people up…who DID NOT SPEAK ENGLISH, and get them on the bus, and off the fairgrounds! But my soon to be ex driver got it done!

Of course, I was the one that had to pay the consequences for letting him use my pass! I lost my free pass privileges to the fair for three years! Ouch! That really hurt. The good news is...after three years, I did get my fair pass back, and the lesson I learned about that is not to let ANYONE else use it!!

Steven Tyler and Aerosmith
At the Men's Club

One night I took Steven Tyler and the Aerosmith band out to one of the men's clubs to eat, since they really do have great food!!

We got to the club and Steven and the guys were given a handful of Funny Money. Funny Money was play money that the club used for celebrities to give the girls so they didn't have to worry about giving them actual money. After they ate, everyone went upstairs to the VIP area to play pool.

While the band was playing pool, all of the dancers were lined up all the way down the stairs waiting to get an autograph. In between shots, the guys were autographing the $20 Funny Money bills and handed them out to the girls.

I'm pretty sure that one night the Funny Money did not get exchanged for cash from the dancers. Those signed Funny Money bills would be prized possessions that would be kept for a long time!

Steven Tyler and the members of Aerosmith were really some exceptionally nice guys and they were always appreciative of the special treatment they were given wherever they went. I always admired and respected that of them!

Super Bowl-CBS Radio

I was friends with the general manager of the CBS Radio stations in the DFW area and was privileged to get to do many things with him and for the stations.

One event I remember well was when the Super Bowl was being held in Dallas. Brian Purdy, the GM called me and told me that he had two or three of the CEOs from New York who were going to be in town for an event at Cowboys Stadium and he wanted me to pick them up at their hotel and take them to the event! I was so fortunate that Brian trusted me to do things that he didn't trust anyone else to do, and this was one of them!

The weather in Dallas during this time seemed to be getting worse by the minute! Of all times for the whole DFW area to be frozen! I picked his guests up at their hotel and made my way to Cowboys Stadium. There was a tent set up out back where the VIPs were to be dropped off. It was about 6 o'clock. When I let them out, I went to a nearby restaurant to eat and wait for the time to pick them up. The sky looked like it could rain or snow at any time!

About 10 o'clock, Brian called to say they were ready to leave. When I walked outside, I was in for a shock! The entire area looked like a big white cake that had been iced in fluffy white icing! Everything was covered in SNOW! The streets were almost empty and there was an eerie quietness about the night!

I was driving my new Escalade and it was probably a good thing that I was driving it! It was higher off the ground so that it made it easier to drive through the snow. The scary thing was that the snow had covered all of the lines in the parking lot, and on the street which made finding where you were supposed to go treacherous! It was a good thing I was familiar with the area around the stadium which made it easier to get back to the tent area to pick them up.

After I picked them up, even getting out of the parking lot was no small feat! Luckily for us, the streets were almost empty which made traveling a little safer not having to watch out for other people who were not used to driving in snow! The dangerous part of the trip was that there was a *layer of ice under the snow*! There were six of us in the car and everyone was helping me watch the road as we maneuvered back to the hotel! It turned out to be a safe, but nerve-wracking drive, even though it was a relatively short one!

My new Escalade proved itself to me that night! I'm sure one of the limos would have made the trip safely, but the Escalade gave me a lot of peace and confidence on the trip!

I want to take this opportunity to thank Brian Purdy, General Manager of the CBS Radio Stations in the DFW area, for having the faith in me to allow me to do things for him that he wouldn't trust anyone else to do. I got to participate in and meet so many interesting people because of him. He once told me that "we are family" and I believed it then, and I still believe it today! Brian, you will forever hold a special place in my heart as a friend and a brother!

Taking the Ladies to Tyler, Texas

When you're in the limo business, you never knew from one day to the next what adventure was going to be coming next!

Late one Friday afternoon, I got a call from one of the strip club owners in Dallas. He was having a grand opening for a new strip club in Tyler, Texas, but he didn't have any dancers! That's really a *bummer* for a strip club! That pretty much defeats the whole purpose of having a strip club!

He had contacted a bunch of girls from one of his clubs in Dallas and had about 20 girls who had volunteered to come dance at the grand opening, and he wanted me to pick them up and get them to Tyler as quick as I could! Of course, Tyler, Texas, is a minimum of 2 hours from Dallas, if the wind is at your back! I agreed, and my son Jeff and I got the limos, picked up the girls and headed to Tyler!

As you can imagine, since these ladies were strippers, some or most of them were pretty scantily clad! They also had several bottles of champagne ready for the trip!

My son, Jeff, is leading the way. And, since we were told to get there as soon as possible, I'm pretty sure that he had the pedal to the metal, as the old saying goes! I know that I certainly did following him!

About an hour into the trip, we saw those dreaded flashing blue lights coming up behind us! I called Jeff and told him to go on, that I would stop and take care of the situation! That was the wrong move! The state trooper was having no part of that! He was mad as an old wet hen and told me to call

163

Jeff and tell him to stop and we would catch up with him! I called Jeff, he did stop, and we caught up with him. In the meantime, we told all of the ladies in the back not to make a sound! We told them do not stick an arm out, don't open the moonroof, do not even whisper! We didn't want any kind of excuse for the officer to want to look in the back since we had two cars full of half-naked, half-drunk women in there! Besides, we were running behind schedule and we didn't need any more delays!

Luckily for us, the trooper took us back to his truck and chewed us out about speeding in *his* district! He was *mad*, and I guess he had a right to be mad since we were *really exceeding* the speed limit! In a few minutes he came back to us and looked pretty frustrated! He told us it was our lucky night, that he only had one ticket left and he couldn't give one of us a ticket and not give the other one of us a ticket! I guess you could say that we dodged the bullet on that one! He gave us a stern warning and sent us on our way, but reminded us that he would be looking out for us on our trip back to Dallas! Yikes!

We slowed down and managed to get our cargo to its destination on time. Jeff and I watched the show and rested up for the trip back to Dallas! It had been a hurry up day and it wasn't over yet!

The grand opening was a great success! The evening was finally drawing to a close. We loaded all the ladies back into the limos for the ride back to Dallas! I told Jeff that we were not going to go one mile over the posted speed limit all the way home, that the state trooper had probably put out warnings about us all the way up and down the interstate! We had dodged getting a ticket one time, but we weren't going to try our luck again!

The trip back to Dallas was considerably longer, but most of the ladies were asleep, and we weren't in a hurry! It's better to take a little longer and arrive alive and without a ticket...than not to arrive at all!

Y'all drive safe out there! And don't speed, at least not through little towns in Texas!

Texas Motor Speedway

April 6, 1997, was the first race at the Texas Motor Speedway! It was located out highway 35W north of Ft. Worth, Texas; pretty much in the middle of nowhere! I was taking a group of people from Lewisville, Texas. To get to the speedway, we had to travel down a small narrow road between Lewisville and 35W. Before I realized it, I ran across a railroad track with a very high crossing level when I heard a loud crash and thud! I stopped the car and got out to see what had happened! As luck would have it, when I hit the railroad crossing, it knocked my muffler off!! I picked it up and put it in the trunk…and off we went. Of course, my beautiful, classy limo now sounded like a loud truck!!! But off we went to the races!!

We arrived at the speedway, and things were *nothing* like they are now! I was able to actually park the limo in the mid-field where the race cars actually were. It was so amazing to watch history in the making! As luck would have it, there was a major pile up in the first turn as the race got started!

Another thing that was so cool about being able to park in the in-field was that as one of the race cars came flying into the area, it stopped about two feet from the limo and where I was standing! You could almost reach out and touch it…as a matter of fact, that is exactly what I did! When I touched the hood of that race car, and felt the power of the engine, I was permanently hooked on car racing! I don't think I have missed one of the races at the Texas Motor Speedway since that time!! If you have never been to a car race like this, the fun and excitement is absolutely unbelievable!

More Texas Motor Speedway Events

*W*orking with the radio stations gave me many more opportunities to work events at Texas Motor Speedway. On many occasions I got to pick up a group of the drivers that would get into town ahead of the races and take them out to eat and to see some shows the night before their teams and families would get into town.

Some of the best places to eat in the Dallas/Ft. Worth area are the gentlemen's clubs. You're probably thinking….I'mr sure men are going there for the *food*…but the food at these clubs is equivalent to almost any 4- and 5-star restaurants. Of course, once they had eaten, there were a few other things for them to *see!* But the food was really why they wanted to go!! Taking certain ones when they came in town for the races became a pretty regular happening!

Also, as pretty much a yearly event, the Speed Zone, which was an entertainment center in Dallas, would sponsor an event with one of the radio stations. They would have one of the race car drivers to come out to their location and have a meet-and-greet with their customers. This gave me another opportunity to pick up a driver from the temporary housing area of Winnebagos at Texas Motor Speedway and hang out a while with the race car drivers and their crew members in their own environments. While being able to do this, it made me realize that their transient life would not be something I would enjoy doing all the time, especially considering the dangerous nature of what they were doing.

On the other hand, when I would just take regular spectators to the races, we still had lots of fun! The rules and regulations were a lot more relaxed than they are now and we would be allowed to go into what I called the "temporary city" where the diehard fans brought their tents and travel trailers and camped out for days before and after the races. I remember one time in particular when the people I had taken to the race wanted to celebrate their birthday after the race. I drove them around the three streets in the temporary city with the sunroof open as they and their guests laughed and sang. We finally stopped and they got out of the limo to cut the cake. Seeing the celebration a lot of the other people gathered around and everyone laughed and partied and celebrated the birthday!

You can be assured that whatever you are doing at the Texas Motor Speedway…you are going to have FUN!!

Watching the Races
from the Suites

Often another perk of working for the radio stations was being able to escort VIPs to the races and staying with them in the suites to watch the race. There would always be more food to eat than you could possibly imagine and all kinds of varieties of foods! There were earphones that you could listen to the race through that blocked out all of the crowd and car noises. Many of the VIPs would be taken down to the starting line to watch the race as it began and I would get to go with them!

I have been blessed to do so many incredible things in my life by being in the limo and transportation business that I would have never gotten to do if I had worked in just about any other business in the world. When I originally thought about starting a limo business, I had absolutely no idea what I was getting myself into….It has been some kind of an AMAZING RIDE!!

The Hulk - Lou Ferrigno

*B*eing in the limo business, when you get up in the morning, you never know what your day is going to bring.

One day, I got a call to pick up someone from the airport and take them to the convention center where there was a body building competition being held. I was to pick up the client at 5:00. Did I mention it was also a Friday afternoon? Five o'clock on Friday afternoon in Dallas is never fun, or fast! However, as was my usual habit, I was there early and waiting for my client! Imagine my surprise when I looked up to see my client walking toward me and he is 6'5" tall...and **even though he is not** *green*, **I recognize him as THE HULK, Lou Ferrigno!!**

We exchanged niceties and then I got him and his suitcase into the limo. As soon as we got into the limo he said, "George, I need to see a doctor right away!" I told him I would take him to the emergency room, but he said no, that he needed to see a private doctor!

I knew by the look on his face and the urgency in his voice that he was completely serious and obviously in pain! Unfortunately, being 5:00 on a Friday afternoon, most doctors offices are closed. I told him I would try to find him a doctor, but I couldn't make any promises!

I made several calls and finally found a doctor that was still open, and she agreed to wait for us to get there. However, her office was all the way across town...on Friday afternoon, at 5:00! As we started to her office, I think I ran a few red lights, did a little speeding, and maybe even cut a few people off (but not too badly)! We arrived at the doctor and they immediately took him back to the exam room. The doctor realized he was in a considerable amount of pain, but she didn't feel comfortable giving him prescription pain medication because she didn't know his medical history, but she did prescribe some good over the counter pain meds! By then it was getting close to time for him to be at his body building judging appointment. We had to rush by the drug store, pick up the medications, and then hurry to the convention center.

When we reached the convention center, it took great effort for Lou to get out of the car. He was still in tremendous pain. I really hated to leave him in that condition, but he assured me he would be alright.

When I picked him up the next day, I could still tell he was suffering! It is terrible when you know someone is in pain and there is nothing you can do for them! Lou and I talked a lot on the way back to the airport and I felt like we became friends. He let me know how much he appreciated me getting him to a private doctor when he first arrived. He told me that he knew I was the kind of person that would try to make a way even though they really didn't see a way. I told him that sometimes you just have to do a lot of praying and watch what happens! And I really do believe that!!

The Other Place
Pride in Our Sports Teams

*T*he Dallas/Ft. Worth area is beyond blessed when it comes to all the sports teams that call it home. I have lived in this area my entire life up to this point and it is really difficult to explain how proud I am to be a sports fan here!

I don't know of another place in the country that has *all* of the different types of sports represented at the professional level that we have! It is incredible to look at the sports history for this area that has been achieved in the past and is continuing even today!

The Texas Rangers have almost won the World Series many times! They are such an elite team that always bounces back no matter what the odds are for or against them!

The Dallas Cowboys have actually won the Super Bowl more than once! They are such an outstanding franchise that they have been branded as *America's Team!* You can't get any better than that! People may not always agree with the way that the owner Jerry Jones runs the team, but one thing that I admire tremendously is his stance on ALL of his players standing for the national anthem! As America's Team, they should show respect for our nation whether any other team does or not! So, I thank Jerry Jones for standing firm on his commitment to honoring our nation!

The Dallas Mavericks won the NBA Playoffs and brought the title to Dallas with its championship team!

The Dallas Stars won the Stanley Cup which is the top honor for the National Hockey League and graced Dallas with yet another top-rated team!

Our soccer teams have also won championships!

These statistics don't even include our semi-pro teams! And the best part of all of it is that every athlete that participate in these great teams contributes something back to their towns and communities! We all benefit from them just being a part of us!

The reason I titled this story "The Other Place" is that most of the world doesn't live in an amazing place like we do that live in the Dallas/Ft. Worth area! So to the world, *we* live in The Other Place; the place where **many things in life are *bigger than life!***

The way I look at it… **"If you're lucky enough to live in Dallas… YOU'RE LUCKY ENOUGH!"**

The Starck Club

*I*n 1984, what would be a very unique and trendy club named the Starck Club was opened in Dallas, the likes of which had not been seen before! It was an old converted warehouse just north of downtown and a nightclub that attracted oil-and-gas scions, southern socialites, gay and cross-dressing men, and boldface names like Rob Lowe, George W. Bush, Princess Stephanie of Monaco, and Maureen Reagan.

When we had clients to take to the Starck Club, it was very interesting! The clientele would typically be dressed up like they were going to a prom or very fancy event! You never knew what your clients would look like on any given night! As you can imagine, there was a lot of laughing and talking among the limo drivers in the parking lot as we waited for our clients to get ready to leave at the end of the night. Typically when someone hired you to take them to the Starck Club, it meant you waited there for them to take them home as well. We usually didn't complain since we were paid by the hour!

The club itself was a two-story structure. From the second floor you could overlook the first level dance floor. However, there were also rooms that were draped off with semi-sheer curtains for a sense of privacy!

A year later, the club unexpectedly found itself at the center of the war on drugs when ecstasy, which was used widely at the Starck, was declared illegal. Some have even argued that the club, which closed in 1989, gave birth to raves — the throbbing, ecstasy-fueled dance parties that became popular in the 1990s.

While it was interesting to 'watch' the people who frequented the Starck Club that never was a place I ever had a desire to hang out or frequent myself. Too many weird things go on in places like that….and personally….I'm not *that kind of weird!!*

The Texas Rangers

*B*aseball has always been one of my very favorite sports. But as much as I love baseball, I love football just about as much. That is one reason that two favorite teams of all time are the Texas Rangers and the Dallas Cowboys! I tell people that I bleed two colors! I bleed red for the Rangers and blue for the Cowboys! However, today, I want to tell you about the Rangers!

It was really difficult for years when it came time for the World Series because we either had to cheer for the Yankees, the Red Sox, or the Dodgers! The team that had my heart was never a contender! I guess you could say that the Rangers playing in the World Series eventually made it to my bucket list!

Like things that usually wind up on your bucket list, you think it is going to take a long time for you to actually see them come to pass. Fortunately for me, the Texas Rangers playing in the World Series came sooner than I had anticipated, but later than I had hoped!

The date was October of 2011! When I knew they were to play in the World Series, I thought I must have already died and gone to heaven! I knew that a lot of very powerful praying people must have prayed for them to have made it that far!

When I look back on that series, I was so honored to be in the stands to get to watch one of the playoff games! Me, Limo George, was watching *My Texas Rangers* play in the World Series! It almost felt like a dream!

During another one of the games, I had driven a group of people there, so I was not able to watch from the stands. Luckily for me, my limo had a hook up for satellite television in it so we could actually watch it on TV. That day the limos were lined up 10-deep in front of the stadium. As long as we heard cheering, and cheering, and cheering, we knew something good was happening! When there was a silence, we knew something not so good was happening! During the loudest cheers, all the drivers would rush over to my limo to look at the TV to see what had just happened! The excitement was so thick you could have cut it with a knife!

It finally came down to one pitch; one pitch! Can you believe I'm saying just one pitch!

With one pitch...we lost the World Series! Even though we lost, it had been such an honor to know that our team was one of the two top baseball teams in the world! They gave it all they had, they were extremely competitive, and we could not have been any more proud of them!

We want you to do it again, Rangers!
We've got your back!

I know that when I get to heaven, members of that team I knew will be there! They were serious about their game and all so good at what they did. I can't wait to see them win that game in heaven...if they don't get another chance to win the World Series down here!

Tiger Woods
Cabaret Royale

I was contracted by the Cabaret Royale to take the dancers to different events that were going on in the Dallas/Ft. Worth area to give out business cards in an effort to solicit business.

One event that I remember taking the girls to was the Byron Nelson Golf Classic. The girls were dressed more like they were going to the beach than they were going to a golf tournament! I personally thought they were beautiful, but I am a man, and I do admire good scenery!

I watched as they walked around the course chatting with the spectators and golfers and giving out business cards. Eventually they spotted Tiger Woods as one of the players in the tournament. Of course, they began flirting and talking with Tiger between holes. I could tell he was totally getting into all of the attention from the dancers. Before the end of the tournament, he had invited them to join him at his hotel. He made sure they had his contact information.

When the girls got back in the limo, they told me where to take them so they could meet Tiger at his hotel.

As they were getting out of the car, they let me know not to wait for them. They would get their own way back to the club! I can assure you that I have no idea what happened that night at the hotel with the dancers and Tiger Woods, but I will just say…. "What happens in the limo (or by way of the limo) stays in the limo!!"